THE
STRAYAN
DICTIONARY

THE
STRAYAN
DICTIONARY

Avo, Arvo, Mabo, ScoMo and all the essential Strayan words

DOMINIC KNIGHT

ALLEN&UNWIN
SYDNEY · MELBOURNE · AUCKLAND · LONDON

First published in 2019

Allen & Unwin
83 Alexander Street
Crows Nest NSW 2065
Australia
Phone: (61 2) 8425 0100
Email: info@allenandunwin.com
Web: www.allenandunwin.com

 A catalogue record for this book is available from the National Library of Australia

ISBN 978 1 76052 935 2

Internal design by Design by Committee
Cover images: BigStock [avocado, sandpaper, cane toad and ugg boots] / iStock [ute] / Shutterstock [beer] / AAP Image/Julian Smith [sausage sandwich]
Set in 12/16 pt ICT Century by Bookhouse, Sydney
Printed and bound in Australia by Griffin Press, part of Ovato

10 9 8 7 6 5 4 3 2 1

The paper in this book is FSC® certified. FSC® promotes environmentally responsible, socially beneficial and economically viable management of the world's forests.

AUTHOR'S NOTE

Please note that many Australian words, customs and people are explored in detail in my previous book, *Strayapedia*—I've tried not to repeat myself, which is why, for instance, this book doesn't have an extremely long and unkind entry on Melbourne, or a detailed explanation of the bizarre history of Vegemite.

This book contains no facts whatsoever, and if anything within reminds you of a fact, you're definitely mistaken. This is all the more true if you're thinking of suing, in which case the passage you object to was ironic, and the words that have offended you should be read as the sincerest praise.

A

Adelaide   The city's bustling North Terrace in 2019

Australia Post   'Postboxes' such as these were once used to send 'letters' instead of emailing them

A.AAARDVARK   The first entry in every category of the Yellow Pages, a business-oriented 'phone book' that was a primitive print version of Google. A.AAARDVARK businesses generally aren't known for their quality, and are unlikely to provide real aardvarks.

A.AAARDWOLF   Inspired by another African animal with an alphabetically convenient name, this is the moniker that el cheapo businesses settle for when someone has already taken A.AAARDVARK.

Abbott, Tony   The 28th prime minister of Australia. His chief achievements were becoming the 28th prime minister, deposing the 29th prime minister, and thereby inadvertently installing the 30th prime minister. Abbott's part in these leadership shenanigans, along with his devotion to opposing action on climate change, and change in general, led him to lose his own seat to **Zali Steggall** at the 2019 election.

   As a private citizen, he now devotes his legendary talent for opposition to railing against his wife's 'socialist' housework roster, while he waits optimistically for a knighthood.

Aboriginal and Torres Strait Islanders   The owners of the entire Australian continent, according to property law, international law, equity, the laws of dibs and the time-honoured rules of front-seat shotgun.

Acca Dacca   A nickname for the band AC/DC which, unusually for an Australian nickname, takes just as long to say as the original.

Adani   Though it derives from India's giant Adani Group and its founder Gautam Adani, in the Australian context the word is shorthand for the proposed Carmichael coal mine in Queensland's Galilee Basin. This would be one of the world's largest mines, and hasten the destruction of the Great Barrier Reef, both through the carbon emissions warming the ocean, and the ships that would transport the coal through the Reef. The ships' damage, admittedly, won't matter quite as much after the Reef is finally dead.

And yet even though the environmental impact would be disastrous, most major international banks have refused to finance it, and coal is dying as a means of energy generation, none of these things matter in comparison to the prospect of mining jobs for a thousand-odd Queenslanders. Plus, as coal mines are becoming so rare nowadays, Adani will no doubt become a tourist attraction that makes up for the visitors lost with the Reef.

Though only just commenced, the Adani project has already provided the environmental movement with some valuable lessons, such as the futility of a bunch of southern greenies marching north to try and stop a job-creating project in Queensland.

Adelaide A picturesque town known as the 'city of churches' due to the large diversity of religious faiths who built houses of worship in the city during its early days, and because Adelaide is still so skyscraper-free that the churches continue to dominate the skyline. Adelaide's vast array of places of worship has also come in handy for funerals over the years, what with all the serial killings.

Nowadays, Adelaide is renowned for its pleasant riverside setting, the fine wine produced in its surrounds, and its cloying social conservatism—non-South Australians may be surprised to learn that in SA, **Alexander Downer** is considered daring and radical.

Every year the renowned Adelaide Festival takes over the city in April, bringing an air of immense excitement, creativity and vibrancy to Adelaide by filling its small CBD with people who aren't from Adelaide.

'Advance Australia Fair' Our national anthem, chosen by a plebiscite in 1977 until it's replaced by something better like 'Waltzing Matilda', 'Locomotion' or 'Khe Sanh'. Even 'Hot Potato' by the Wiggles would be an improvement.

Among its many problems is that a country that is home to the world's oldest surviving culture is hardly 'young', while the word 'free' is the height of irony for a former penal colony—and then there's 'girt'. The original lyrics of Dodds McCormick's ditty also contained some fairly nauseating lines about 'true British courage', very little of which was on display during all the massacres of Indigenous Australians.

The main virtue of 'Advance Australia Fair', however, is that it is not 'God Save The Queen'.

Aerial ping-pong A supposedly dismissive nickname for Australian Rules football, although in truth, the idea of table tennis played in mid-air is extremely exciting and cool, and anyone going to an AFL game expecting aerial ping-pong is likely to be disappointed.

Afterpay A revolutionary Australian financing system that, by spreading payments across eight weeks, makes it easier for people across the world to purchase things they can't really afford.

Albanese, Anthony The leader of the **Labor Party**, as at the time of writing. He's known as a heart-on-sleeve true-believer type, so much so that he once even wept during a press conference over Kevin Rudd's removal, to the surprise of everyone who remembered Kevin Rudd.

Albanese is an unusual choice for Labor's leadership because he hails from the party's left, or the too-idealistic-to-win faction. Consequently, despite being elected unopposed, the right's superior talent for machinations means that he's unlikely to be Labor leader by the time this book comes out.

This would be an unwise political assassination—like many that the Labor right have attempted in recent years—as 'Albo' shares with the late **Bob Hawke** a jocular likeability and a universally used nickname. The overwhelming sense that he'd be a good person to go on a pub crawl with, although hardly a demonstration of fitness for office, is probably his best hope of getting elected, especially when it's remembered that most of his colleagues are either entirely unknown or actively disliked.

In contrast, Albo is so quintessential an ordinary Strayan that his middle name is Norman. This has rendered him a stark change from his predecessor **Bill Shorten**, who has long had a reputation as the kind of guy who wouldn't bother to backstab you when he could knife you in the face.

So far, it's unclear what Albanese's policy plans are, besides abandoning much of Shorten's policy platform, which was extremely detailed, surprisingly progressive and a massive electoral liability.

In recent years, Albo has become known for his DJing, which is somehow both pretty cool and deeply irritating.

Aldi   A German discount supermarket that is now widespread across Australia, Aldi is notable for producing tribute-band equivalents of many beloved Australian grocery brands, often in packaging so similar that lawsuits have followed. Its deliberately small-format stores offer an extremely limited range, displayed extremely simply, often in just a cardboard box, and have proven popular because this severe lack of options allows customers to finish their shopping in just a few minutes.

One of Aldi's most famous initiatives is its racks of seemingly random 'Special Buys', which allow shoppers to fill their homes with temporarily available items they absolutely do not need at prices so inexpensive that their customers simply can't resist an alpaca grooming kit, a waterproof snowmobile cover or a home proctology set.

A recent article in the *Sydney Morning Herald* claimed that ukuleles and paint-your-own rock kits had both been unexpected bestsellers for Aldi, illustrating the virtue of the retailer's trademark 'throw shit against the wall and see what sticks' approach to its range.

The biggest driver of Aldi's stunningly rapid success in the Australian market, however, is its range of high-quality, low-cost booze. These products do not always achieve the same quality and flavour as their more expensive competitors, but never fail to make customers just as drunk as the name brands.

Allcott, Dylan   As a world number one tennis player and a winner of multiple grand slam events, and also a gold medallist in basketball, as well as a successful triple j presenter and TV host, and the founder of a music festival, Dylan Allcott is the most phenomenally talented person in Australia, especially as all of these things were accomplished in a wheelchair. And yet he's less famous in this country than Sam Newman.

More disappointingly still for the versatile star, he won a Logie for most popular new talent in 2019, an accolade that has a long track record as the Australian television industry's kiss of death.

Aly, Waleed   As a public intellectual, columnist, author and legal academic, Aly is the most overqualified person to host a programme on the network that gave us *Huey's Cooking Adventures*.

Aly is the second most unlikely person ever to be awarded the Gold Logie, behind Norman Gunston who not only wasn't a real person, but even more improbably, was on the ABC. (**Tom Gleeson** is the third most unlikely, because even though he's a smartarse on the ABC, he's nevertheless a white man, like the vast majority of Gold Logie laureates.)

Infuriatingly, Aly is also an awesome rock guitarist, who once played a flawless rendition of the solo from 'Comfortably Numb' at the Walkleys. He will probably someday become the first UN secretary-general to launch a worldwide fundraising appeal accompanied by a witty graphic presentation and his own fingerpicked version of 'Tears in Heaven' on a blue acoustic guitar.

Ambo Ambulance officer. This characteristic Strayan abbreviation saves precious milliseconds in emergency situations.

Andrews, Kevin The Liberal member for Menzies, first elected in 1991 which makes him 'Father of the House', the honorary title given to the longest-serving Member of the House of Representatives. As a conservative, family values–upholding politician, Andrews would want to clarify that he is not literally the house's father, as he is not married to it. This 'Father' is resolutely pro-life, though on the evidence available, seems not to have had much of one.

Marriage in fact gave Andrews his most notable moment during his long years in the parliament, when as **Tony Abbott**'s social services minister, he introduced a scheme offering $200 vouchers for marriage counselling. Only 13 per cent of them were ever taken up, perhaps because Andrews did a photo shoot to publicise them in which he and his wife are pictured sitting a long way apart on a sofa, holding hands but looking into the camera lens like startled raccoons.

Andrews is probably pleased that his signature coun-selling vouchers were subsequently abandoned—while embarrassing for him at the time, they would now have to be made available for same-sex marriages, which he has long opposed. It's not clear whether his marital advice to same-sex spouses would be to stick together to preserve the institution of marriage, or that they should divorce to minimise the potential for sinful sexy times.

Despite his staunch Christian views, however, Andrews attempted to show insight into other religions in November 2017, when he proposed a law designed to protect freedom of religion that would have allowed 'Islamic bakers' to refuse to bake cakes for Jewish weddings, and vice versa. This attempt to promote mutual discrimination between two other religions backfired, as Muslim and Jewish bread-makers united in their refusal to rally behind Andrews' banner.

Although currently a backbencher, Andrews has an extremely favourable view of his own leadership potential, though one which appears not to be shared by his colleagues. He mounted an unsuccessful leadership spill against **Malcolm Turnbull** back in 2009, shortly before **Tony Abbott** succeeded in his own spill.

Andrews also ran for deputy leader in 2015, losing to **Julie Bishop**, and in 2016 grandly announced he would be willing to challenge Turnbull again, undermining the then-prime minister just as he was due to go to the polls. No doubt Andrews remains ready to serve if required, and will not be.

Anning, Fraser   A former senator who briefly gave Australians the distinction of having elected a white supremacist to our federal parliament, Anning achieved the challenging feat of making One Nation seem restrained and moderate.

Though he was spectacularly disloyal to Pauline Hanson's party, quitting it immediately after being sworn in as their new senator following **Malcolm Roberts'** disqualification, Anning remains true to the cause of the tiny, hateful minority of white people who are terrified by immigration and want it stopped. As a senator and then as a candidate, Anning carried their torch as though he were attending a far-right rally, and said similarly hateful things.

Anning gave his maiden speech in the Senate after joining Katter's Australian Party, and called for a 'final solution' to immigration, to widespread disgust and disbelief. Hanson herself described Anning's speech as 'straight from Goebbels' handbook', which it can only be hoped was intended as a criticism.

It took Katter, who initially praised the speech, several months to figure out that he really should expel Anning from his party, a process which may well be considered rapid by the convoluted standards of the North Queenslander's brain.

Anning went onto form his own 'Fraser Anning's Conservative National Party', borrowing and amalgamating two existing party brands, yet still failing to win many voters as by the time of the election, his name wasn't exactly a strong selling point. This was largely thanks to a speech during the campaign where he blamed the Christchurch massacre on Muslim immigration—that is, its victims.

In response, the would-be new glamour boy of the Australian far right had an egg broken against his head by a teenage school student, Will Connolly. In doing so, the student who soon became known as Eggboy, was acting on behalf of millions of Australians who didn't know they wanted Anning egged until it happened.

In response, Anning punched Eggboy in the head several times, because he has a great sense of humour and is a total sweetheart.

Winning a mere 1 per cent of the Queensland Senate vote in 2019, Anning proved that while quite a few Australians may well be 'a little bit racist', very few of us are willing to vote for someone who is blatantly so.

Ant's pants A phrase meaning 'great', which presumably evolved because of the rhyme instead of anything particularly special about the notion of trousers for ants, which would be impractical.

Not to be confused with Antz Pantz, an Australian underwear brand indelibly associated with the phrase 'Sic 'em, Rex'.

Apple A global tech company known for innovation, progressiveness and aesthetic excellence.

— **Apple Isle** Tasmania, known for the opposite.

— **Apple Store Federation Square** Ditto (and consequently abandoned).

— **Apples** The phrase 'she's apples' means everything is fine. Though scholars claim that it's an example of rhyming slang, where 'apple and spice' stands for 'nice', it's just as easy to believe that in rural Tasmania, a certain narrowness of life experience might have left orchard farmers with difficulty imagining anything better than a lady who is constituted of apples.

Archibald Prize Australia's most iconic art prize, even though Brett Whiteley once won it with a portrait of a crazed baboon being handed a syringe. The Prize's long-standing popularity derives from the thousands of visitors who attend each year specifically to get angry about the judges' decision, and instead vote for their 'robbed' favourite in the People's Choice section.

It is an axiom that any painting which wins the Packing Room Prize, awarded by the foreman in charge of unpacking the entries, can never win the overall award, making it the worst prize to win in the art world.

Arthur or Martha To 'not know whether you're Arthur or Martha' is a phrase used to indicate uncertainty. At a time when Australians are increasingly aware of the challenges associated with gender dysphoria, it's probably best abandoned.

Arvo 1. Afternoon, abbreviated because who can be bothered saying the extra syllables when they're relaxing on a sofa in the arvo? In cases of extreme laconicness, 'sarvo' is used, meaning 'this arvo'.

2. How **wankers** say **'avo'**.

Asia Pacific Triennial One of the country's most significant contemporary arts events, taking place at the Queensland Art Gallery and Gallery of Modern Art, and attended by many artsy and cultural types from across our region. Pauline Hanson would hate it if she'd ever heard of it.

Atlassian   A multibillion-dollar, NASDAQ-listed software company that is based in Sydney, proving that it's possible for Australians to start phenomenally successful, global tech companies without needing to relocate to Silicon Valley, even though they're the only ones who've ever managed to do it.

The most extraordinary aspect of Atlassian's success is that they've managed to convince highly skilled tech-industry professionals from around the world to relocate to Australia despite the NBN.

Atlassian's products are used primarily for collaboration, or e-**mateship**, and the company's billionaire founders Mike Cannon-Brookes and Scott Farquhar are so dedicated to their own offline collaboration that they recently moved into adjacent harbourside mansions in Sydney.

Aussie   Australian, because what could be more Aussie than abbreviating a word with an 'ie' or 'o' suffix?

The abbreviation is also used to signify the Australian dollar. Given recent brutal exchange rates, Australians travelling overseas generally accompany this usage with a swear word.

— **Aussie Aussie Aussie, Oi Oi Oi**   A popular Australian war cry, often heard at sporting events. Most war cries have lyrics and rhymes—Australians have chosen not to bother with such frippery, opting instead for an abbreviation and a grunt.

Australia   The name of the country evolved from the Latin phrase traditionally cited at the bottom of European maps—*terra australis incognito*, meaning 'unknown southern land'. That means that even the name of this island continent is a reflection of European ignorance about the many millennia of Aboriginal inhabitation.

The choice of 'Australia', which was championed by Matthew Flinders and Lachlan Macquarie, also set the country up for years of confusion with 'Austria'. Still, it's a better name than 'New Holland'.

Australia Day   A national holiday celebrated on 26 January, the day when Captain Arthur Phillip's First Fleet landed at **Sydney** in 1788. It is not the day Australia was first settled, or came together to form a nation, or commemorating a moment of nationwide significance, or marks indeed anything besides a bunch of unwanted **Poms** arriving in Sydney Cove on boats and intending to stay, an action which is both illegal and the worst possible taboo in our society today. Even the name '**Australia**' was not adopted for many years after 1788.

26 January was also the day on which Australia's traditional Indigenous owners were legally dispossessed, and marks the commencement of a struggle that continues today. However, pointing out these historical antecedents and consequently suggesting that a better, more unifying date should be found has become yet another front in Australia's now-perpetual culture war, and is considered tantamount to treason by many of our most irritating commentators.

If rather than the date being changed, the day were renamed 'Sydney Day', 'British Day' or 'Boat People Day' to more accurately reflect the event that it commemorates, the desire to find another date for our national holiday would become instantly overwhelming.

26 January is also the author's birthday, and he is willing for the holiday to be used for a nationwide celebration in his honour instead.

Australia II   The boat that won the America's Cup yacht race in 1983, sparking a fanatical yet brief period of nation-wide interest in yachting. The victory marked an end to 132 consecutive years of victories by the New York Yacht Club, the longest winning streak in sporting history, and would have been an even bigger achievement had it not been accomplished in the sport of yachting.

A key element in *Australia II*'s success was the winged keel designed by Ben Lexcen—the very sporting Americans mounted a legal challenge to this innovative design, which is one of the reasons why Australia's eventual victory felt so utterly satisfying.

After *Australia II* won, the prime minister **Bob Hawke** suggested a national day of **sickies**, and was so cheerfully boisterous during the celebrations while wearing such a hideous patriotic jacket that he was impossible to defeat in every federal election he contested thereafter.

During the next race in 1987, the San Diego Yacht Club immediately won the 'Auld Mug' back from the defending Australian yacht *Kookaburra III*. No Australian boat has made the final since, while New Zealand yachts have won it twice since 1983. Not coincidentally, America's Cup races are no longer treated as front-page news in Australia.

Australia Post   Australia's national post office, which has long been dedicated to delivering letters all over this enormous country with remarkable speed and efficiency. But now that nobody sends letters anymore, Australia Post has evolved to focus primarily on delivering parcels from Amazon, eBay and THE ICONIC, while its letter deliveries have increased in price and dropped off in volume to the point where they should start marketing themselves as a 'premium product' where a real human being hand-delivers your PDF.

Australia Post's national network of post offices has also refocused their offering from archaic post-related services to novelty gifts, discount highlighter sets, prepaid credit cards and other knick-knacks that **Aldi** rejected for their super specials. Their branches always have dozens of varieties of USB drives on offer at each cash register, as Australia Post unwisely stockpiled the last product that sought to replace paper stationery, only to see Dropbox render them obsolete as well.

Avago   A demand that somebody 'have a go', often paired with 'ya mug'. During **Scott Morrison**'s prime minister-ship, 'avinago has become a precursor to 'gettinago.

Avo   Avocado, because 'cado' is just so onerous to say.

It was suggested by the social researcher Bernard Salt that young Australians couldn't afford to buy property because they blow their disposable income on '**smashed avocado**', which is now the preferred way of serving avocados at fancy cafés, often on a wooden board. As one of the many baby boomers who has profited enormously from the massive increases in real estate value, pricing millennials out of the market, Salt was fortunate that the understandable backlash to his article didn't lead to him getting smashed himself.

a2 Milk A milk company which worked with the Australian dairy industry to develop a herd whose milk does not contain the supposedly problematic A1 protein. Their patented research also found a way to add 50 per cent to the price.

B

Beer snake   A rare sighting in the wild *(Martin Pot)*

Bunnings   The busiest department of the Warehouse in Nelson Bay

Barangaroo An ambitious project to remove the ugly container terminal at the north-west edge of Sydney's CBD, and restore the natural shoreline so that the harbour can lap against a rocky outcrop once again, just as it did when the First Fleet arrived.

This has now been accomplished, and builders are proceeding with the second stage of the plan, and will ruin the area afresh by building ugly office towers and a massive, intrusive casino.

Barbecue Both the high point of the nation's cuisine, and its most important social occasion. Barbecues are enjoyed by all, as enough alcohol is generally consumed for attendees to ignore the habitual overcooking of the steak and undercooking of the sausages. This generally occurs because the man who insisted on taking control of the barbecue after triumphing in a primitive dominance ritual has also consumed a large volume of alcohol.

— Barbecue apron Garments known for the hilarious messages printed on them, which constitute the apex of Australian humour. Popular apron witticisms range from 'kiss the cook' to 'my drinking team has a rugby problem' to rubber breasts, which are especially amusing when worn by corpulent men.

— **Barbecue stopper**   A topic so significant that it would immediately hijack any other discussion at a barbecue. As used by politicians, its biggest and only fans, the term radically over-estimates the level of interest in politics at an average Australian barbecue. In truth, the discussion at any given barbecue centres around housing prices, sport, and the price of housing near major sporting venues.

'Bart vs Australia'   The episode from Season 6 of *The Simpsons* where Bart visits down under after causing a fictional diplomatic incident with Australia. The stereotype-filled episode, which mocks the imaginary Paul Hogan-style image that American viewers would have presumed reflected reality, caused a genuine diplomatic incident with Australia—the episode was condemned in the actual Australian parliament, which is the scene of the episode's annoying climax.

The episode's producer David Mirkin now claims that the episode was designed to be as infuriatingly inaccurate as possible, a goal that was achieved spectacularly. It should be noted that he and the other people responsible for the episode have yet to visit the parliament for a ritual kicking from the Australian prime minister.

A petition to change the name of the Australian dollar to 'dollarydoos' failed to achieve its end despite achieving nearly 70,000 signatures, thank God.

Barty, Ash   A Queensland tennis player who has adopted a radical approach to the game for a contemporary Australian player by being really good at it, and making no fuss whatsoever.

Barty was hailed as a promising junior, having won the junior Wimbledon title, but felt excessively pressured as an adult, which led her to take a break from tennis and play Big Bash League cricket despite never having played the sport competitively before, an odd method of clearing her head. However, getting her mind off one high-pressure competitive sport by playing another one evidently worked for her, as Barty then returned to tennis and won the French Open before becoming number one in the world, just like her mentor Evonne Goolagong Cawley, and unlike any of the much-talked-about Australian men currently playing on the circuit.

Indeed, Barty's no-fuss, high-competence approach has perplexed **Nick Kyrgios** and **Bernard Tomic**, who cannot understand how she has performed at such a high level without destroying racquets, abusing linesmen and accruing code violations.

Bastard   Though the word traditionally means somebody born out of wedlock, in Australia the term is used as a compliment or insult depending on the context—both usages have proven confusing for visiting *Game of Thrones* fans. It should be noted that the term '**pommy** bastard' is never a compliment.

Bathers   Swimmers.

Battler 1. Someone of limited financial means who struggles hard to better themself.

2. Someone of comfortable financial means who views themself as hard done by because most of their disposable income goes on their foolhardily large mortgage.

— **Howard's battlers** People who voted for John Howard because they shared his belief in enterprising Australians doing it for themselves without the interfering government getting in the way, and who were subsequently lavishly rewarded by his middle-class welfare programmes.

The baby bonus, first home owner's scheme, private health insurance tax rebate, Family Tax Benefits, Senior Australians Tax Offset and other lavish payments really helped battlers to pay their own way like the self-reliant **Aussie** champions they were.

— **Little Aussie battler** A common phrase since the 1970s, the addition of 'little' adds an appropriately patronising note to battlers' heroic self-mythology.

Beer While rum was initially used as the de facto currency in New South Wales, beer soon replaced it, and has remained in this exalted position ever since. Beers are bought in a round for **mates**, handed out by the slab as a thank you, and brought to parties as six-packs as a form of compensation before the guest consumes most of their host's collection of top-shelf spirits.

— **Beers** What many Australians say when inviting friends out for a drink, lest inviting someone to 'go for a beer' imply that they're some sort of soft loser who would only drink one in a session.

— **Beer bong** A tube connected to a funnel used not to inhale marijuana, but to consume a more socially destructive drug.

— **Beer snake** An enormous slithering creature native to Australian cricket grounds. An admirable example of plastic recycling in action, beer snakes have recently become an endangered species due to the ordering limits imposed by responsible drinking legislation and overpolicing by serpent-hating grounds staff.

　　Unlike most Australian snakes, they are not poisonous, except to the livers of those who contribute too enthusiastically to their formation.

— **Murder a beer** 'I could murder a beer' means 'I'd really like a beer', not that a person wants to do violence to a beer. Regrettably, however, violence is known to occur after the consumption of beers.

Beetroot Long **milk bar** tradition dictates that for a burger to be deemed 'Aussie', it must contain a slice of tinned beetroot that stains the bun bright purple. The other mandatory ingredients are lettuce, tomato, cheese, onion, pineapple and a fried egg, which successfully covers most of the major food groups, allowing the consumer to erroneously believe that eating a burger is a healthy choice.

　　This broad selection of toppings, along with lashings of barbecue sauce, became widely adopted in the Aussie burger recipe because of the growing realisation that tinned beetroot tastes like fermented dirt.

— **Beetrooter** A nickname for the crimson-visaged politician **Barnaby Joyce**. It's assumed that while he's in the throes of sexual ecstasy, for instance when fathering yet another child, his face turns even more purple than usual.

Benaud, Richie The only person in Australian cricket since the World Series Cup era to achieve genuine gravitas. As low a bar as that is, Benaud will always be remembered as much for his gentlemanly dignity as for his iconically mangled pronunciation of the number 'two'.

As a player, Benaud was invaluable for combining two rarities—a leg-spinner, and a genuine all-rounder—and was a successful captain as well. Benaud may have been famous for wearing beige, but he never was it.

Bewdy A Strayan pronunciation of 'beauty', generally used to signify that something great has happened. There is not a strong association between Strayan words and any kind of aesthetic beauty.

— **You bewdy** An even more emphatic expression of delight that is not meant as praise for anyone's physical appearance, except perhaps that of a winning racehorse or greyhound.

Bex A traditional Australian painkiller that was apparently only effective when combined with a cup of tea and a nap. Since Bex originally contained phenacetin, which is now known to be carcinogenic and cause kidney disease, the remedy sometimes caused more problems than it solved.

One famous recent use of the phrase was when Kevin Rudd responded to questions about him potentially challenging his successor Julia Gillard by saying that everyone should have a 'Bex, a cup of tea and a good lie down', instead of what he should have said, which was 'Yes, I totally am challenging her, so there.'

Shortly after Rudd's unsurprising challenge succeeded, he lost the 2013 election, partly due to his habit of making annoying, antiquated references.

BHP Broken Hill Proprietary, a major mining company that was once known as 'the big Australian', until it became much bigger and much less Australian. Its merger with the UK-based Billiton saw it follow the time-honoured antipodean tradition of hanging out in London, doing a little bar work, and ultimately coming back home when things didn't work out—consequently, the company is now known just as BHP.

The company's namesake in its Western NSW town of origin is now a considerably more broken hill, thanks to BHP mining it until it no longer existed. Nevertheless, as one of Australia's largest companies, BHP has a proud record of job creation both at home and in Papua New Guinea, where its Ok Tedi mine created a huge amount of work for those helping the 50,000 local people affected by the pollution that BHP caused.

Big Bash League Australia's premier Twenty20 cricket competition, played by women and men. The name has the double meaning of a big hit of a cricket ball and a big party, and unlike most football codes, tends not to involve actual bashing. Since its inception, the men's competition has been sponsored by a brand strongly associated with athletes at the pinnacle of their physical fitness, KFC.

Big Kev The human equivalent of a **Big Thing**, Kevin McQuay was a larger-than-life salesman on breakfast television, known for his lurid shirts, corpulent physique and white hair that resembled a cross between **Bob Hawke**'s famous bouffant and a sulphur-crested cockatoo. Big Kev's catchphrase was 'I'm excited', which was certainly apparent in his hugely enthusiastic presentation, but seems impossible in hindsight given that he was talking about cleaning products.

— Big Kev the brachiosaurus One of the few full-sized model dinosaurs in Australia not owned by **Clive Palmer**, the 18 metre Big Kev was a local landmark on the Stuart Highway near Darwin, a location almost as desolate as Palmer's abandoned Palmersaurus theme park at Coolum.

Big smoke A large city. In Britain, the phrase is thought to be derived from London, which was once encrusted with soot and covered with smog; in Australia, however, the phrase is thought by some to have Indigenous origins. Nowadays the phrase feels anachronistic, as the centres of our biggest cities are some of the few places in Australia that aren't susceptible to horrific bushfires.

Big Things Oversized versions of common everyday items, constructed in the generally forlorn hope that tourists will flock to visit them. The better-known big things range from the Big Banana at Coffs Harbour, to the Big Merino at Goulburn, to the Big Ugly Pile Of Pink And Grey Rocks at Federation Square.

Billabong   1. Globally renowned surfwear brand.

2. A Wiradjuri word meaning a watercourse that fills only after rain.

3. An ideal place for a jolly swagman to drown himself after being caught stealing livestock—presuming the watercourse is full at the time. If not, poetically haunting the billabong afterwards is likely to prove difficult.

Bills   A global restaurant chain run by its namesake, celebrity chef Bill Granger. Despite the punctuation, there is only one Bill. He has been forced by his publishers and producers to use apostrophes in the names of his books like *Bill's Basics* and TV shows like *Bill's Food*, however, which must frustrate him enormously.

From his origins in a small corner café in Sydney's Darlinghurst, Granger has expanded to Japan, South Korea, the US and the UK. Curiously, Bills (respecting his disdain for apostrophes) global empire is based on scrambled eggs, probably the dullest dish ever to become a celebrity chef's signature.

Granger's menus always feature these eggs, along with his ricotta hot cakes and corn fritters. While the rest of his menus are extensive and ever-changing, blending elements of Asian and other world cuisines with a consistent emphasis on fresh, high-quality produce, most visitors ignore them and just get eggs on toast.

Billy   A bush teapot, originally made from an empty tin of 'bully beef', and generally stoked in a campfire. Later usage commemorates the prime minister Billy McMahon, whom many Australians also wanted to throw in a fire.

Bindi   1. A weed with sharp barbs that can transform an ordinary lawn into a minefield for barefoot children.

2. A children's entertainer who has often been the subject of sharp barbs.

Bishop, Julie   The obvious person to succeed Malcolm Turnbull as prime minister, due to her great popularity and the widespread praise for her performance as foreign minister. But due to the peculiar internal dynamics of the Liberal Party, anyone with huge personal support who supports popular centrist policies must be crushed ruthlessly, especially if they have the audacity to be female.

Black armband view of history   An accurate view of Australian history.

Black Stump   Used as a marker for the end of civilisation in the phrase 'beyond the black stump', which signifies a remote, middle-of-nowhere place. It is also the current location of the once-popular Black Stump steak restaurants.

Bligh, Anna   A former Queensland premier whose trajectory from Labor leader to CEO of the Australian Banking Association would have caused considerable shock had it not happened at the same time as Mark Latham's even more extreme departure from the Labor movement.

Bligh's loss of the 2012 state election was the most comprehensive defeat of any Queensland government, but far from the first time that a Bligh has been dramatically turfed by those underneath them.

Blind   1. Highly intoxicated, as in absolutely farken maggoted.

2. Unable to see due to problems with one's eyes, rather than just being blind drunk.

3. A device for covering windows, preventing light from entering. This is highly useful in the event of someone having been blind drunk the night before.

Blinky Bill   Dorothy Wall's beloved 1930s books told of the adventures of a 'quaint little Australian' anthropomorphic koala. Yet the popular children's character wallpapered over the tawdry reality of koala life, which is largely devoted to a crippling eucalyptus addiction, the contraction and transmission of chlamydia, and napping.

The books also had a strong conservation message, which has been entirely ignored by several generations of readers, with the result that koala populations have continued to plummet.

Blood worth bottling   Saying somebody's blood is worth bottling is a great compliment. It's unclear precisely what system of blood-bottling the idiom envisages, however— how would the blood be collected? Would somebody maintain a central store of the bottled blood of admirable people? For what purpose? And why would anybody distinguished be willing to supply their precious blood cells to such a vampiric museum?

It might be sensible to update the idiom by saying that somebody's genes were worth replicating.

Bloody   1. An expletive used for emphasis, often equivalent to 'very', as in 'It's bloody hot'.

2. Covered in blood. This usage is most common in **Adelaide**.

— **Bloody hell** A common Australian expletive indicating surprise. **Scott Morrison**'s Tourism Australia used it in an ad starring Lara Bingle, where she asked potential tourists 'Where the bloody hell are you?' When they watched the advertisement, most Australians also reacted by saying 'bloody hell'.

— **Bloody oath** An expression of affirmation, which generally does not require anyone to cut themselves and swear an actual oath.

— **Kevin Bloody Wilson** Not a bushranger or serial killer, but a comedian. Whether somebody finds the name 'Kevin Bloody Wilson' amusing is a useful predictor of how entertained they'll be by his comedy.

Blowie Originally an abbreviation for 'blowfly', the word now encompasses another activity associated with blowing and flies.

Bludger A person who does no work. The term originally referred to a pimp—as in, someone who lived off another's earnings—who carried a club used to bludgeon clients who were remiss in handing over the cash. It's unclear whether JK Rowling knew of this more sordid meaning when she used the term in her books to refer to the balls that fly repeatedly at quidditch players' heads, propelled by beaters.

By contrast, an Australian bludger would simply drop to the ground and do nothing.

— **Dole bludger**   A person receiving unemployment benefits. Many Australians find themselves perfectly able to
look down on welfare recipients while simultaneously
espousing their belief in the '**fair go**'. The view that
people on welfare are dole bludgers is precisely why
Newstart is still so abominably low—so inadequate, in
fact, that anybody living on the modern version of 'the
dole', which gives recipients around $40 a day, would
not find life much of a bludge at all.

Bluey   1. A traditional traveller's swag, which was historically wrapped in blue blankets.

2. A nickname for a redhead, allegedly hilariously
because their hair isn't the least bit blue.

3. An ABC children's programme about a blue heeler dog
called Bluey and her friends. The show is highly successful
around the world thanks to the universality of its themes
and the humour with which they're explored, with the
result that overseas viewers are finally discovering that
Australia makes children's television shows that aren't
Skippy.

Bogan   A derogatory term for lower-class Australians.
Bogans may be identified by their flannelette markings
and mullet plumage, and are found mostly in **Macca's** car
parks, sitting on the bonnets of the highly polished V8s
they like to collect as trophies.

Bogans undertake an annual migration to Canberra for
a ritual known as the '**Summernats**', and are considered
an endangered species thanks to their prodigious consumption of Winnie Blue cigarettes.

— Cashed-up bogan Australian sports star.

Bogut, Andrew An Australian basketballer so good at the game that he was the first pick in the 2005 NBA draft, and won the championship ten years later, before returning home to Australia at the end of his playing career.

In 2019 he had the surreal experience of being signed from the Sydney Kings, who play to less than sell-out crowds in Homebush, back to the Golden State Warriors, who almost defended their NBA championship with Bogut as an integral part of their playoffs team.

More bizarrely still, Bogut then decided to return to Sydney to honour the second year of his contract with the Kings.

Bogut is less accomplished as a political commentator than as a basketballer, however, having once tweeted comments that suggested he found the Pizzagate controversy credible—that is, the discredited theory that senior members of Hillary Clinton's campaign were part of a child sex ring based at a Washington DC pizzeria, which led one gun-toting idiot to shoot up the pizzeria. The scandal that followed Bogut's comments required every bit of his defensive mastery.

Bondi tram To 'shoot through like a Bondi tram' is to accelerate rapidly, as the express trams from the city to Bondi used to do. The phrase makes little sense in contemporary Australia—the line was dismantled in 1960, so Bondi trams are more accurately described as fatally shot than shooting through. It is curious that the phrase has remained in circulation, as all modern methods of transport to Bondi Beach are agonisingly slow.

Bonzer   A slang word meaning 'great' that no Australian still uses unironically. Some people think it derives from 'bonanza', others from the French 'bon', while many others feel it doesn't matter, as the word doesn't seem all that bonzer anymore.

Boochani, Behrouz   An Iranian-Kurdish writer who has been detained in Australia's detention centre on Manus Island since 2013. He fled Iran after several of his colleagues at a magazine promoting Kurdish culture were imprisoned by authorities—a situation one might think justifies a grant of political asylum, and yet he's still there. His memoir *No Friend But The Mountains* was composed via a series of text messages, and surprisingly contains no emojis.

Boochani's book won prizes at both the Victorian and NSW Premier's Literary Awards in 2019, which regrettably hasn't helped the slightest bit with his struggle to improve the lot of Manus detainees—indeed, he wasn't even able to attend the awards.

While the minister, **Peter Dutton,** has the discretion to offer him an Australian visa at any time, it's thought that Boochani cannot qualify, as he is unwilling to work as an au pair for a wealthy Liberal Party donor.

Boofhead   An idiot, and especially an uncivilised one. See also **Folau, Israel**.

Bottle   Being the 'full bottle' means being good, genuine or expert. This is because Australians love and respect nothing more wholeheartedly than a full container of alcohol.

— **Bottle-o**   A bottle shop, and of course one where the bottles in question are full of alcoholic drinks. Bottle-os are treasured sites in Australian society, viewed as something like a combination between a pharmacy and a temple.

Bottom of the harbour   A tax avoidance scheme where companies were stripped of their assets and scuppered like an abandoned ship, meaning that tax authorities were unable to recover the money they were owed. It was banned by legislation in the 1980s.

It's important to note that the phrase is a metaphor, and that the most prominent scheme involving the literal bottom of Sydney Harbour, the Sydney Harbour Tunnel, is not included—although like the illegal bottom-of-the-harbour schemes, it has cost taxpayers a large amount of money, due to motorists avoiding it and the government having to make up the shortfall to its investors.

Bradbury   To 'do a Bradbury' is to succeed only due to the failure of others, in honour of Winter Olympics short track speed-skating gold medallist Steven Bradbury, who won a magnificent default victory when the other three finalists crashed into each other.

While the victory appeared a total fluke to those not familiar with the intricacies of speed-skating, it's such an absurdly dangerous sport, featuring such frequent crashes, that Bradbury's strategy of hanging back behind the leaders was actually quite sensible, arguably unlike his decision to compete in speed-skating to begin with.

Australians have subsequently figured out how to win Winter Olympic gold medals without the need for other contestants' collective self-destruction, but Bradbury remains an inspiration to all who have won their positions with a degree of dumb luck while their opponents took one another out—a group that now includes the Australian prime minister.

Branch stacking   The traditional Australian method of winning preselection. This is made easier due to the generally low membership of political parties in Australia, and is made easier still by the customary inclusion of votes from dead people.

Brass razoo   A coin, as used in the phrase 'he doesn't have a brass razoo', which suggests that the person in question is very poor—a usage that dates back to WWI. Since most experts agree that there has never been a coin known as a 'brass razoo', it's correct to say that nobody has ever had one.

Brown, Bob   Revered by tree-huggers across the country for his tireless campaigning to save the Tasmanian wilderness and subsequently for his role in the foundation of the Australian Greens, which he then led for many years. His departure has left the Greens largely in the wilderness.

Buckley's   'Buckley's chance' means no chance at all. The original Buckley whose hopelessness led to the phrase is unknown, which is consistent with what people said about his luck. The phrase has survived despite the Brownlow Medal-winning efforts of Nathan Buckley for the Collingwood Football Club, a team that has Buckley's chance of ever losing its status as the game's most hated team.

Bucks Dollars. As we merely imported an American name for our currency, it made sense to lazily import their nickname, too.

Budgie smugglers Brief male swimwear. It's not known whose genitalia bore a sufficiently close resemblance to a small domestic bird for the term to become widespread.

The term was popularised in recent years by **Tony Abbott**, who is known for wearing red budgie smugglers—though in his case, he's more likely to use them to conceal a raw snacking onion.

Speedos were famous as the iconic Australian purveyors of budgie smugglers, but then they got taken over and their headquarters moved to Nottingham, where their swimwear is now used to smuggle finches and robins instead.

Bundy and Coke The most distinctively Australian mixed alcoholic beverage features a local product, Bundaberg Rum, being overwhelmed by something cheap, mass-produced and American. Like many an inhabitant of regional Queensland, most of the rum's production has moved to Sydney.

Bundy Rum's mascot is a polar bear even though its hometown is in quite a warm part of Australia, a decision that seemed funny at the time to a group of people who had consumed a lot of Bundy.

Bunnings   Originally a big-box hardware chain, Bunnings is now best known as a retailer of charity sausages which are so popular that mountains of spare ingredients have to be kept in large warehouses adjacent to the barbecue. Despite the chain's enormous sausage turnover, the company insists on using gormless untrained workers in its ads instead of actors.

Bush   The parts of Australia where there are no people but lots of trees. This is by contrast with the outback where there's not much of anything.

— **Bush week**   The phrase 'What do you think it is, bush week?' has irritated the author since childhood, and for the record, he has once never thought that it was bush week. The term is presumably a sneering reference to periods when countryfolk attended the agricultural shows in the cities.

— **Bushie**   Someone who spends a lot of time in the bush. The phrase implies some basic level of bushcraft and survival, though no non-bushie would have any way of knowing whether someone purporting to be a bushie had any such skills, a dilemma illustrated in the movie *Crocodile Dundee*.

— **Gone bush**   When someone has 'gone bush', they have taken off into the great outdoors. The phrase is never used to refer to pubes.

Bushfires   The Australian term for forest fires, bushfires are natural processes that have shaped the continent since time immemorial, and will never be able to be prevented entirely—except for those bushfires lit by firebugs, which represents most of them nowadays.

During the colder months, anything resembling a bushfire is probably a hazard reduction burn, an event that allows rural fire management authorities to create fire breaks that reduce the chances of deadly bushfires, while also significantly increasing asthma attacks.

Byron Bay   A relaxed and peaceful beach town in Northern NSW, 'Byron' is now so famous that the town centre is perpetually packed with irritating backpackers, which makes both residents and non-backpacker visitors quite stressed.

Cape Byron is the eastmost point on the Australian mainland, which is really trippy to think about if you've bought shrooms from some dreadlocked dude you met in the common room of your hostel.

— **Byron Bay Writers' Festival**   One of the best literary events in the country, loved by all who attend, and gratuitously mentioned here in the hope that the organisers will invite the author.

C

Cane toad A young toad ponders which ecosystem to devastate next
(*Bidgee*)

THE LANDING of the CONVICTS at BOTANY BAY

Convicts Prisoners who were found guilty of theft disembark to a stolen
country

Cab sav   An informal nickname for the cabernet sauvignon wine variety, which makes Australians feel more relaxed about swilling such a posh-sounding beverage from a goon bag.

Cactus   Something that is 'cactus' is not working, broken or useless. This usage seems rather unfair to cacti, which perform their admittedly limited function of being spiky in deserts with a high degree of reliability.

Canberra   The capital of Australia, a monument to bad compromise since 1913.

— **Canberra bashing**   Attacking our national capital, even though all it ever tried to do was provide an over-planned location for political infighting and more roundabouts than anybody could want. (For a thorough example of Canberra bashing, see the author's *Strayapedia*.)

— **Canberra bubble**   A phrase Scott Morrison deploys when he doesn't want to answer a question, asserting instead that the topic in question would only be of interest to the kind of lame nerds who play close attention to politics, instead of the 'normal' **quiet Australians** he serves, who don't mind what he does unless he bothers them by doing a Bill Shorten and attacking their franking credits or negative gearing. Unlike most bubbles, the Canberra variety has consequently been rendered opaque.

A subject being 'inside the Canberra bubble' is no reason not to answer a question about it, of course, seeing as every decision that affects the nation gets made inside that same theoretical bubble—whose centre is the parliament where Morrison is paid to be our most senior representative.

Morrison adopted a similar tactic as Immigration Minister, refusing to discuss 'on-water matters' as though scrutiny of his portfolio were only possible on dry land. His perceived success in the portfolio illustrated the surprising truth that there is nobody who can make a minister answer questions from the media if he's shameless enough to simply refuse to do so.

It's thought that Morrison's oft-stated fondness for '**quiet Australians**' is driven by their tendency not to ask questions.

Cane toad   A poisonous toad with a voracious appetite for both food and **shagging**. Cane toads were introduced to North Queensland in an attempt to control the cane beetle infestations that were devastating the sugar crops. The toads performed brilliantly, but at the expense of creating a worse pest problem, as cane toads are prolific breeders, extremely hardy and highly toxic even to humans.

'Cane toad' has become a nickname for Queenslanders in general, perhaps because they are also a blight on the landscape.

Captain's pick   1. In sport, a decision that is the captain's exclusive right to make.

2. In politics, a decision unilaterally and often spontaneously imposed by the leader despite the misgivings of their colleagues, which almost always turn out to have been worth listening to. Captain's picks tend to lead eventually to the removal of the very authority used to impose them—as in Tony Abbott's ultimately suicidal decision to bring back knights and dames. Before long Abbott found himself out of the job he cornily referred to as 'Captain of Team Australia'.

Carlton Zero   A new alcohol-free beer-like soft drink from Australia's biggest brewery, Carlton Zero makes the brave assumption that Australians are interested in drinking beer for its flavour instead of that thing where it makes them drunk.

Cashless Welfare Card   A system of providing welfare to vulnerable citizens via a debit card that can only be used at merchants with appropriate card facilities, and cannot be used for alcohol or gambling purposes. The programme offers participants a basic level of sustenance in return for their autonomy and dignity.

Cassidy, Barrie   A political journalist who somehow managed not only to get people to wake up early on Sunday mornings, but to spend that time watching *Insiders*, a show about politics. He also managed to stave off a challenge from a competing programme hosted by Andrew Bolt, an altogether less surprising achievement.

Census   The mandatory survey of Australians that takes place every five years and provides the government with the statistical information it needs to plan vital public services. However, during the most recent census in 2016, it emerged that the government had been unable to successfully plan the census itself. The ABS website crashed for much of the evening, leading to justified doubts about whether our bureaucrats would do a decent job of planning any of the government's other services. Ultimately, many people simply filled out the census on paper.

Subsequent surveys of the Australian people found a near unanimous view that the Australian Bureau of Statistics had done a shithouse job of planning an event with five years' notice.

Chairman's Lounge   Often called Australia's most exclusive club, the Chairman's Lounge is a network of secret Qantas airport hideaways where senior business executives, politicians, celebrities and other Very Important Customers get to consume fancy meals and expensive booze while they hobnob and hope for free upgrades.

The legend of the Lounge took a substantial hit, however, when it was revealed that the former senator and current national blight **Fraser Anning** was a member. While he was immediately kicked out by the airline's CEO after his hateful comments about Christchurch, it hurt Qantas' reputation considerably when it was revealed that they were his preferred airline for white flights.

Chardonnay socialist   A rich and therefore self-contradictory left-winger. The term is an adaptation of the British 'champagne socialist', and dates from when chardonnay was a marker of a comfortable middle-class lifestyle. Nowadays, chardonnay can be bought as a cleanskin at Dan Murphy's for $4.99 a bottle, so the phrase should be updated to 'craft beer socialist'.

Checkout chick   A demeaning label for a female super-market worker. Given supermarkets' inexorable shift towards making customers scan their own groceries, however, we are all checkout chicks now.

Chewie   1. Chewing gum.
2. Chewbacca from *Star Wars*, who is superior both in terms of flavour and nutritional quality.

Chiko Roll   A spring roll-like cylindrical snack whose major ingredients are cabbage, grease and greasy cabbage. Despite the name, and indeed the fact that it was originally called the 'Chicken Roll', it contains no chicken—although it does contain both beef and beef tallow, whatever that is. The fact that the Chiko Roll remains legal and is apparently widely consumed illustrates just how far Australia is from solving its obesity crisis.

The Chiko Roll as we currently know it debuted in Wagga Wagga in 1951, in an effort to construct a meal that could be eaten with just one hand. In the 1970s, 40 million were sold per year in Australia, making the Chiko Roll the most successful product to be developed in Wagga Wagga, and also the only successful product to be developed in Wagga Wagga.

Chook   A chicken. Australia's most famous chook was Graham 'Chook' Fowler, a corrupt police detective from **Kings Cross** who was filmed taking a paper bag of cash in the front seat of his car during the Wood Royal Commission. Nowadays, many Cross locals are nostalgic for the days when their suburb had enough nightlife to support organised crime and police corruption.

— Chk Chk Boom girl   Another person who rose to widespread notoriety in Kings Cross.

Christmas Island   An external territory of Australia that follows Australian law and is governed by an administrator appointed by Australia's governor-general despite being just 350 kilometres from Java. Its citizens vote in federal elections, receive the same TV channels and share Australia's +61 telephone prefix. But anyone trying to claim asylum there will discover that for that purpose only, it is not considered part of Australia's **migration zone**. Indeed, following the perceived effectiveness of Christmas Island's excision, the whole mainland was ultimately excised as well.

It is part of Australia, though, for the purposes of detention centres, one of which was opened there under the Howard government, closed in 2018, then reopened by the Morrison government just before the 2019 election, costing millions of dollars. It was then closed after the election before any asylum seekers could be sent there, which really must have seemed like Christmas to the lucky service providers. It will no doubt be reopened when next deemed politically expedient, presumably just before the 2022 election.

In recent years, the Australian government has opted to conduct most of its immigration detention on another birdshit-filled phosphate island that is more clearly not part of Australia—**Nauru**.

Chunder   To indulge in the most characteristically Australian form of self-expression, vomiting. The word is so treasured that it features in Men At Work's iconic song 'Down Under', largely because 'chunder' is one of the very few words that rhymes with 'under', and they'd already used 'plunder' and 'thunder'.

Clacker   A slang term for the anus that emerged, perhaps surprisingly, thanks to classical education, as it derives from the Latin 'cloaca'. Its most famous usage in recent years was undoubtedly in the *NT News* headline 'Why I Stuck A Cracker Up My Clacker'.

The cloaca is also the defining characteristic of mono-tremes like the platypus and echidna, as they have only one opening for urination, defecation and reproduction, providing an exception from the common Australian saying 'Up the bum, no babies!'

Clayton's   A fake or inferior substitute, derived from a once-popular soft drink that was served in a container resembling a whisky bottle and marketed with the slogan 'The drink you have when you're not having a drink'. The name has survived long after the product has disappeared because of the lingering fury most Australians who tried it experienced after taking a swig of something that looked like an alcoholic drink but wasn't.

Cobber An antiquated term for a mate, which is now rarely used without irony. It's thought by some experts to have its origins in the Yiddish word 'chaber', meaning comrade. Not all Jewish people have reported being embraced here quite as warmly as this word might imply.

Cocky A somewhat dismissive term for a small-scale farmer. 'Cocky' is thought to be an abbreviation of 'cockatoo', and reflects the contempt that early European settlers with larger holdings felt for those less successful than them. The cockatoo analogy supposedly arose from a perception that small-scale farmers devastated plots of land like a flock of ravenous cockatoos.

Of course, nowadays small-scale farming is highly trendy, especially when used to supply pretentious locavore restaurants. Some committed inner-city foodies even grow fruit and vegetables in their tiny balcony gardens, which are located in places where pollution and deforestation guarantee that there aren't any cockatoos to ravage them.

Cold Chisel A band that is one of the rare musical success stories to come out of Adelaide, which only occurred because they did in fact come out of Adelaide in order to move to Sydney.

'Chisel' experienced long-term success both in terms of their many hits, and the other members' success in convincing frontman Jimmy Barnes to scream less on their recordings than he went on to do in his solo career. Despite having a Scottish singer, the band is quintessentially Australian, as is evident from the group's failure to make it big overseas, and also because it's named after a tool.

The group was once the biggest live act in the country, however, and famously had 10 per cent of Darwin's population at one of their shows, although the band members nevertheless outnumbered the audience.

As a testament to their enduring popularity, Chisel have now spent more years doing nostalgic reunion tours than the six astonishingly productive and notoriously wild years they originally spent together as a band.

Coles A supermarket chain that somehow survived the decision to use Status Quo in its marketing, Coles has in recent years appealed to lovers of the environment by banning single-use plastic bags, and haters of the environment by releasing zero-use plastic 'Little Shop' replicas of its products.

Convict Australians with British colonial heritage. Convict labour was responsible for many of the early buildings in the colonies, and this may be why Australian governments still have a nasty habit of suppressing building and construction unions.

Ironically, many Britons today voluntarily transport themselves to Australia because of the superior lifestyle, while young Australians often punish themselves with a few years of low-wage jobs in London before finishing their cruel sentence in oppressive conditions and coming home.

Cooee 'Come here' in the Dharug language of Western Sydney. The Dharug people called out the highly resonant word to find one another in the bush, back before texting was a thing. Noticing that the sound travelled well over great distances, Europeans copied the custom, promptly ruining it.

Cordial A sugary drink that Australians once convinced themselves was suitable for children because a kid in the ad said that his dad picked the fruit that went into it.

— **Coola cordial** A luminous green cordial produced by Cottee's that is described as 'lime', but isn't fooling anyone. It's allegedly Australia's favourite cordial flavour, a rare aberration in a country known for its strong foodie culture.

   The ingredient list of Cottee's Coola flavour contains sugar, water, food acid (citric acid), flavour, preservatives (sodium benzoate, sodium metabisulphite), colours (tartrazine, brilliant blue FCF). Cottee's marketing materials have never specified which kid's dad picks the tartrazine and the sodium metabisulphite.

Corner store In some suburban areas, corner stores provide a range of useful items that save locals from driving to the supermarket—from basics like milk and bread to groceries, flowers and services like dry cleaning pickup, making them the hearts of their neighbourhoods. These days, however, corner stores are being replaced by convenience stores, which offer their customers a poorer range, less personal service and higher prices, along with disturbingly intense neon lighting. And where corner stores were once run by members of the same family, who got to know their clientele on a first name basis, convenience stores are invariably staffed by an ever-changing roster of bored, unmotivated teenagers. The change has yet to prove more convenient.

Cossies   Togs.

Crabb, Annabel   An ABC presenter known for the extreme bravery she displayed not just by interviewing politicians, but by sitting down to share lengthy meals and engaging in hours of small talk with them on her show *Kitchen Cabinet*. She somehow accomplished this without ever stabbing a single federal representative with a kitchen knife.

This extraordinary gift for patience is also visible in her friendship with her podcast co-host Leigh Sales, despite the latter's propensity to burst into show tunes.

Cricket   Once a sport associated with the upper classes and genteel decorum, and renowned for taking a leisurely three to five days per game, modern cricket is played by **cashed-up bogans** who are in it for the money and prioritise the new forms of the game that are over in a few hours, but earn them millions.

In modern cricket, the only time that the game's traditional politeness is displayed is when players front the media to make a mandatory apology.

— **Cricketer**   Someone adept at hitting, bowling, fielding or tampering with a cricket ball.

— **Cricket captain**   The on-field leader of a team. The position of Australian cricket captain has been said to be more important than that of prime minister, and in recent years it has been almost as unstable.

— **Cricket Australia** The organisation charged with the sacred responsibility of looking after the beloved game on behalf of its loyal fans, and which generally doesn't.

— **'It's not cricket!'** Originally used to imply that something was untoward, the phrase has turned full circle, and now means that something is free of endemic corruption.

Crocodile Dundee A romantic comedy movie about a **larrikin** bushman from the Australian outback who falls in love with a journo from New York City, and is amusingly out of place when he visits her home town. *Crocodile Dundee* was a global hit and did terrific things for the Australian film industry on the world stage, while at the same time doing terrible things for the image of Australians on the world stage.

Most people who saw the film were unable to conceal their disappointment when the **Aussies** they subsequently met never shaved with a machete, were unable to hypnotise cattle and/or muggers using one hand, and as residents of one of the world's most urbanised countries, weren't at all out of place in big cities.

Crook The use of this abbreviation of 'crooked' as an adjective meaning 'bad' is distinctively Australian, as is ringing to tell the boss you're 'a bit crook' after a big night. Given how many Australians have convict heritage, it's surprising that the word doesn't just mean 'normal'.

Crowe, Russell An actor who is originally from New Zealand, but has lived in Australia for many years. Crowe was nominated for the Best Actor Oscar for three years in a row, for *The Insider, Gladiator* and *A Beautiful Mind,* winning only for the worst of those roles.

The actor still isn't an Australian citizen, despite how often we try to claim him—he has said that he applied and was knocked back twice, while the immigration department claims he never applied at all. One would think that this could be sorted out with a phone call, at least if Crowe could restrain himself from throwing the phone.

Giving Crowe citizenship would also allow Australia to share and thereby ruin NZ's only ever moment of Best Actor glory, which is an excellent reason for the government to make it happen.

'Crowie'—note the Australian nickname—also deserves to be considered Australian for his long and largely thankless stewardship of the South Sydney Rabbitohs rugby league team, who at one stage found themselves out of the competition entirely, and then only a few short years later found themselves with an excessively supportive owner who insisted that they wear Armani suits when off the field.

Crowe was ultimately rewarded with an NRL premiership in 2014, although it's unclear whether they won because of the passion that saw him regularly regaling the team with poetry recitals, or because the team's management promised that every time they won a game, they wouldn't have to listen to any poetry.

There are of course drawbacks involved with Crowe becoming an Australian citizen, such as every aspect of his musical career, from his early days as Russ Le Roq to his various bands with the acronym TOFOG. Perhaps

Australia should instead cut a deal whereby New Zealand keeps its bragging rights over Crowe and all his success, but Australia takes over full ownership of Neil Finn.

Culleton, Rod Once a senator for One Nation, Culleton's brief time in the federal parliament will be remembered only for its end, when his election was invalidated by the High Court for two entirely separate reasons—a bankruptcy and a criminal conviction. Culleton's decision to represent himself presumably failed to help his cause.

Despite this very clear determination of his status, Culleton continued to call himself @SenatorCulleton on Twitter for many months after his involuntary departure, and was rumoured to have been spotted in the parliament wearing a home-made lanyard which one suspects would not have survived the scrutiny of a court either.

Culleton ran in the 2019 federal election for the 'Great Australian Party', and the High Court's decision to exclude him from the Senate was emphatically confirmed by WA voters.

Not to be dissuaded by the unhappy realities of democracy and mathematics, Culleton has now launched his own YouTube channel where he explains why the original Australian Constitution Act passed in the UK has been violated because the Queen is no longer the Queen of Great Britain in Australia, or something—the author tried to watch one of the videos and quickly got as confused as Culleton seemed to be at his court hearing.

Rod Culleton will run for the Senate again some day, no doubt, because in his heart he knows that he is still rightfully a senator, no matter how often he's told that he definitely isn't.

Cummings, Bart   Despite winning the Melbourne Cup a remarkable twelve times, the greatest achievement of the trainer they called the 'Cups King' was breeding and sculpting his even more remarkable eyebrows.

Currency lad/lass   Someone with British heritage who was born in Australia. The term was originally used by British-born Australians as an insult, since 'currency' was a term used to refer to coins from other countries that were in circulation in the Australian colonies alongside pounds sterling. The term was ultimately abandoned when it became evident that Australian-born people weren't the slightest bit interested in looking up to anybody just because they were born in Britain—a view that only hardened when air travel made it possible for more Australians to visit Britain.

D

Dutton, Peter   Despite concentrating desperately hard, he still isn't sure how many votes he has *(Australian Embassy Jakarta)*

Darwin   Mitchell Street is Darwin's main nightlife strip, relatively speaking *(Bidgee)*

Dag   1. A dried piece of sheep poo. Dags tend to stick to wool, requiring them to be removed by someone known as a 'dag-picker', which is probably the worst job in Australia besides being **Ray Hadley**'s producer.

2. Someone who isn't very fashionable, perhaps because they wear jumpers with clumps of sheep faeces still stuck to them.

— **Rattle your dags**   A request to hurry up, presumably because rattling a sheep's hindquarters would dislodge multiple clumps of poo, thus hurrying up the dag-picker's job. The other kind of dags can be made to hurry up by telling them that ugg boots are on special.

Daks   Trousers. However, to 'dak' someone means to remove their trousers. Consequently, the question of whether someone is wearing trousers can sometimes be ambiguous, a conundrum most notably illustrated by former prime minister Malcolm Fraser during a visit to Memphis, Tennessee.

Damper   Unleavened bread traditionally baked in the smouldering ashes of a fire. This was a staple for **bushies**

during the early days of British colonisation, but despite its romantic campfire origins, there is no need to eat it now that both yeast and sliced bread are readily available.

Dark Mofo   A winter festival in Hobart curated by the Museum of Old and New Art. It has been embraced by Tasmanians and their government despite its name being an edgy abbreviation for 'motherfucker'. It's thought that this is because Tasmanians either aren't aware of the abbreviation, or see no problem with that kind of thing.

Darwin   The capital of the Northern Territory is named after the famous naturalist because the NT's rates of alcohol consumption are so prodigious that a night out drinking in Darwin subjects the drinker to natural selection.

Darwin was devastated by Japanese bombers in WWII and then Cyclone Tracy destroyed most of the city's buildings in 1974, but each time Darwin was rebuilt, because its residents remain utterly devoted to their remote, croc-infested, boozehound-filled city.

David Jones   As the department store chain's famous slogan puts it, there's no other store like David Jones, except Myer.

Daylesford   A spa town north-west of Melbourne, Daylesford was first established as a gold-mining town, but is now entirely devoted to the mining of mineral water.

Democracy sausage   The most indispensable element in Australia's political system, the 'democracy sausage' is purchased on election day at local primary schools, where it is always served on home-brand supermarket white bread with a squirt of tomato sauce and, if it's one of those fancypants schools, a bit of fried onion.

These election day fundraising sausage sizzles have transformed citizens' obligations under Australia's compulsory voting system into treasured opportunities to eat delicious greasy snags, and maybe even a **lamington**. Those who suggest an end to compulsory voting are generally ignored, as it's widely feared that a reduction in voter numbers might lead to some polling places failing to provide the electoral snags that are every Australian's birthright, requiring hungry citizens to head to their local **Bunnings** instead.

Democrats, Australian A centrist party devoted to 'keeping the bastards honest' until it was comprehensively defeated by those bastards.

Devon A processed luncheon meat that has also been known as 'fritz', 'polony', 'stras', 'Belgium', 'Windsor sausage' and 'German sausage' in different areas of Australia, due to apparent ignorance about where the meat comes from— although in fact, it's a perfect example of why nobody should ask questions about how sausages are made.

These quirky regional language differences will ulti- mately be defeated by the emerging national consensus that nobody should eat gross processed luncheon meat.

Didgeridoo A musical instrument originally from Arnhem Land. While the term may sound to non-Indigenous people like a word that originated in an Aboriginal language, many experts believe that the name in fact came from white people attempting to imitate the sound of the instrument, in some cases insultingly. This derivation is depressingly plausible.

In recent years, woke white people have attempted to embrace the sound as 'really cool' and started calling the instrument a 'didge', which is also highly problematic. There can be no better illustration of this scourge than the Jamiroquai songs 'Didgin' Out', 'Didjarama' and 'Didjital Vibrations', which are irritating even by the standards of Jamiroquai in general.

In recent years, the instrument has increasingly been known as the '**yidaki**', which is the name used by the Yolngu people from whose country the best-known form of the instrument comes. Let's use that.

Digger An Australian soldier. The term originated in World War I, where troops spent much of their time digging trenches, which is an apt illustration of the brutal boredom of that conflict. On the other hand, digging trenches was far safer than being ordered out of them.

The term is still used today, even though Australia's modern soldiers are trained to operate military hardware that is far more complicated than the shovel.

Dinkum Correct, of integrity. Its origins are debated, but *Ozwords* has concluded that it was originally an English dialect word meaning 'work'—often with the sense of doing a fair amount of it. Indeed, their article about the word's origins is so long that it must have taken a great deal of dinkum to research—and through this example we can see that 'dinkum' no longer bears that meaning today.

— **Fair dinkum**   Being 'fair dinkum' is the highest compliment an Australian can pay to someone or something's integrity. Fair dinkumness is an unimpeachable guarantee of quality and probity, similar to a AAA credit rating. It also has a secondary sense of being in accordance with prevailing social standards, and specifically, Australian ones—perhaps surprisingly for a word that is fair dinkum **Pommy**.

— **Dinkum oil**   Accurate information, a usage which evolved during World War I when the troops on the ground were kept without much official information, and rumours were rife. Consequently, soldiers would frequently ask one another for 'the dinkum oil', although they rarely got it.

   A growing awareness of its environmental impacts has led to the realisation that oil itself cannot be considered dinkum.

Dob   To inform on one's mates, to be a tittle-tattle. This is the greatest social crime an Australian can commit, and will immediately eradicate any perception of **dinkumness** that they may have attained. The taboo against dobbing possibly dates back to convict days, and probably limits the effectiveness of law enforcement, just as the Mafia code of Omertà does. That said, the consequences of dobbing tend to be far less fatal.

— **Dobber donkey**   A person known for dobbing. It seems unkind to associate donkeys with this most cardinal of Australian sins, since the term seems to arise from the overlap of letters at the start of the words, rather than any informant tendencies observed in donkeys.

Donkey vote Australia's preferential voting system requires voters to decide which representatives they'd prefer if their first choice is rejected by other voters, a selection process that the donkey vote bypasses by simply numbering the boxes in order from top to bottom.

The term 'donkey' implies idiocy, but it can be conceded that voting does seem less important now that the prime minister we elect is never permitted to finish their term.

The donkey vote is common enough that being placed first on the ballot is considered beneficial, but it occurs far less often than the donger vote, where the elector simply draws a penis on the ballot paper. That is considered an informal vote, both because it's not valid for the purposes of the election, and because one should not expose one's genitals at formal polling places.

Dorothy Dixer A Question Time inquiry made by a member of the government to one of their own ministers, leading to a scripted speech full of tedious boasting. The only interesting thing about them is their origin, as Dorothy Dix was a syndicated advice columnist suspected of writing her own questions.

Dorothy Dixers guarantee that only half of Question Time is entertaining, while the other half is so excruciating that it's genuinely surprising that visitors sitting in the public gallery don't strangle themselves with their lanyards.

Downer, Alexander A former Liberal leader who is in some respects Australia's Boris Johnson, given his privileged origins, time in the foreign affairs ministry, and penchant for verbose gaffes.

The two also have in common that they were once discussed as potential prime ministers. In Downer's case a gaffe rapidly ended that possibility, whereas in Johnson's case his gaffes only improved his chances, to the point where he now holds the office. It's not known whether Johnson enjoys dressing up in fishnet stockings, as Downer once did for a photo in a magazine, but given his Etonian background, it seems perfectly plausible.

From 2014 to 2018, Downer served as Australia's High Commissioner to Britain, in which capacity he played an unlikely role in the Trump–Russia scandal, as the person whose drinks with Trump campaign official George Papadopoulos ultimately led to the Mueller investigation.

After the meeting, Downer sent a diplomatic cable to Canberra saying that he'd gained the impression from Papadopoulos—who was later imprisoned for making false statements to the FBI—that the Russians were helping Trump against Hillary Clinton. The revelation that drinking with Alexander Downer can lead to a prison sentence has reduced the perceived desirability of socialising with the former Liberal leader from what was already a low point. Previously it was believed that the major danger involved in spending time with Alexander Downer was having to spend time with Alexander Downer.

In 2018, Downer was replaced because the government managed to find someone even more pompous and gaffe-prone to serve as High Commissioner—George Brandis.

Drongo   An insult akin to idiot, believed to be derived from a racehorse called Drongo that never won a race in 37 starts, a winning percentage comparable to that of the St Kilda football club. The horse was most likely named after a family of tropical birds, represented by the spangled drongo in Australia. Spangled drongos are also common at the Eurovision Song Contest.

Drop bear   A terrifying bush creature that drops down from trees onto the shoulders of unsuspecting bush-walkers, whom they attack and sometimes even devour. The fanged drop bears are as ferocious as their koala cousins (let's forget briefly that koalas aren't bears) are placid, and definitely exist despite the rumours that they were invented as a practical joke on American servicemen and other tourists. After all, Australia is full of so many terrifying, deadly creatures that it seems unlikely that anybody would need to invent another one as a joke.

Dropkick   1. Kicking the ball after letting it bounce first—an important skill in both rugby codes, as well as for soccer goalies, and of no use in any other situation.
  2. A loser, such as someone who climbs Uluru after being expressly asked not to by its traditional owners. Even more massive dropkicks are those crowds of tourists who flocked to Uluru for the express purpose of climbing it before the October 2019 deadline.

Dunny   A slang term for toilet, originally used in Australia to refer to outdoor conveniences, which nowadays tend to feel more like inconveniences. Dunnies are known for being freezing in winter throughout much of the country, and, between the user's exposed flesh and the dunny's dark, damp environment, are the perfect location to experience the Australian tradition of being bitten by a redback spider.

Dusty, Slim   A legendary country music singer who abandoned his perfectly pleasant birth name of David Kirkpatrick to instead embrace two adjectives. Dusty was known for his uniquely penetrating insight into the darkest fears of ordinary Australians, most notably when he sang a song about a pub with no beer. Subsequent songs such as 'The Answer To A Pub With No Beer', which detailed the pub's problems with the brewery supply chain, and 'The Sequel To A Pub With No Beer', which explained how air freight was used to improve supply, failed to resonate quite as deeply with listeners.

Dutton, Peter   Minister for Home Affairs in the Coalition government, as opposed to **Barnaby Joyce**, who was Minister for Work Affairs.

Formerly Dutton was a Queensland police officer, and member of the Drug Squad. As a politician, whether joking about rising sea levels or commenting that Malcolm Fraser's decision to allow Lebanese Muslim migration was a mistake, Dutton displays every bit of the sensitivity and respect for civil liberties for which Queensland cops have long been renowned.

As one would expect from a minister with so much power in such a broad and crucial portfolio, Dutton has a reputation for never exaggerating a situation for political opportunism, trying always to act on the deep commitment to restraint and respect for the rule of law that have long served as his lodestar.

He would never dream of victimising an ethnic minority to project a sense of crisis designed to undermine the Victorian **Labor** government's re-election, for instance. Though many felt his comments about African gangs ahead of that election were inappropriate, Premier Daniel Andrews greatly valued his involvement, as the intense backlash it produced was politically beneficial for Labor. Further, it must be noted that Minister Dutton adores many ethnic minorities, especially white South African farmers.

However, Dutton's most noteworthy achievement was his attempt to challenge the prime minister who had only recently entrusted him with such a powerful ministry, **Malcolm Turnbull**. Dutton's attempted coup faltered when he was unable to secure enough support to replace the PM, leading to him being outmanoeuvred by **Scott Morrison**, whose candidacy was largely reactive. Dutton's retention of his seat at the 2019 election is most likely due to a similar miscalculation by voters in the seat of Dickson.

This was not Dutton's only problem—as has become apparent in the round of Coalition bloodletting that followed the 2019 election, had Dutton succeeded in deposing Turnbull, the former prime minister would have advised the Governor-General that there were eligibility questions that might have prevented Dutton from assuming office. This is because of concerns about the Dutton family childcare business, which it has been argued received funds from the federal government, which might have violated constitutional eligibility provisions.

And yet, ignoring the question of whether Dutton is even eligible to be an MP, who better than Peter Dutton to care for a child? Unless that child is an asylum seeker in Australian custody, of course.

E

Engadine McDonald's The management would probably be fine with not being Australia's most famous fast-food restaurant *(Maksym Kozelnko)*

Eurovision Guy Sebastian represents a country thousands of kilometres from Europe *(Ailura)*

Earbash To talk at length, oblivious to your interlocutor's obvious desire to escape. While the term is generally used to describe a one-on-one encounter, at times an entire nation can be earbashed, as occurred in 2010 when the independent MP Rob Oakeshott took an extraordinary 17 minutes to announce who he was supporting as prime minister on national television, a task he could have accomplished in two words. Nobody ever listened to Oakeshott again.

Economic rationalism An Australian term to describe a situation when governments make decisions primarily by taking financial factors into account, implementing free-market policy without regard for human consequences. The approach generally works very well for the economy, but not so well for many of the humans who have to try and survive in it.

The approach is even more problematic when governments refuse even to act on what would make sense economically, but instead implement dogma that has been proven not to work, like giving lots more wealth to rich people in the belief that it will magically trickle down to poor people.

Emu bob A name which makes the activity described— picking up litter in a group—sound much more interesting than it is. In fact, 'emu bob' sounds like a version of apple bobbing, except with enormous native birds picking up the fruit instead of humans—as opposed to humans trying to pick up emus with their mouths, which would not go well.

The name was inspired by emus' habit of bobbing their heads down to the ground when they eat, an activity which is objectively nothing whatsoever like picking up a discarded cheeseburger wrapper with your hand.

Ian Kiernan and Kim McKay founded the nation's largest emu bob, known as Clean Up Australia Day, and eventually expanded the concept to Clean Up The World Day, which takes place in September each year. It can safely be assumed that the concept would never have gone global if it had been called World Emu Bob Day.

Engadine McDonald's A branch of the giant burger chain that's famously popular with local rugby league fans, including some neighbourhood celebrities. Using their restrooms when the Sharks are in the grand final is not recommended, and some of those in attendance may not even make it that far, instead having to settle for their own **daks**.

Esky A plastic box which keeps food and drinks cold. The Esky was invented by a company called Malley's, because of course one of the few enduring Australian inventions is a device to keep beer cool.

One of the great virtues of the Esky is that not only does it stop your stuff from getting warm, but you can sit on it while enjoying its contents.

Eurovision Song Contest An annual event where weird singers from Europe compete—more weirdly still— against Australia. It seems that Australia was allowed to compete because, in yet another example of the organisers' inability to detect irony, the Eurovision team thought our love of their batshit crazy song competition was genuine.

Expat An expatriate Australian. Over a million Aussies are thought to be overseas at any one time, and many of them are living and working in places like London, New York, LA, Hong Kong and Singapore—and that covers 99 per cent of them.

Since most of these places are in the Northern Hemisphere and freezing at Christmas, expats generally migrate home during the winter, where they regale their friends and family with tales of how wonderful their lives are in some of the world's most exciting cities. These claims are somewhat undermined by how enthusiastically the returned expats rush each day to the closest Australian beach in an effort to make their skin appear less pasty, and organise lengthy drinking sessions that are mandatory for their old, non-expat friends to attend.

Most expats intend to return home when their children are in school, because as wonderful as their new lives are, they want their kids to grow up with Australian accents, and 'spend time with their grandparents'—which really means that they are hoping to benefit from free childcare.

Exxy Expensive. Given the cost of living in its major cities, this term can be used to describe the majority of Australia's populated areas. Admittedly, those who live in cheaper regional and rural areas pay a price in other ways.

F

Fairy bread Children should rest assured that the bread contains no fairies whatsoever

Funnel-web The Sydney variety—which Melburnians insist is nowhere near as good as the Victorian funnel-web *(Fir0002/Flagstaffotos)*

F45   A global chain of gyms founded by Australians, F45 has the unique market position of being much more expensive than regular gyms, while offering a smaller space and less equipment. As against that, F45 boasts Mark 'Marky Mark' Wahlberg among its investors.

In any case, its popularity is skyrocketing globally, which is probably due to F45 offering new functional (hence the 'F', which does not stand for 'Funky Bunch' despite the involvement of 'Marky Mark') training routines every day, each lasting for only 45 minutes, which apparently solves most people's major bugbear about gym attendance—its repetitive dullness. The other benefit, supposedly, is that everyone works out together as a team, which allows the group's fittest members to judge the slobs more cruelly.

Nevertheless, F45's adherents are so passionate, and so dedicated to telling others how much they love F45 and how they should totally join, and that in fact there's a special eight-week programme with a special price coming up, that it may ultimately be recognised as a religion and given an appropriate tax exemption.

Fair go A phrase beloved of both sides of politics despite its quaint antiquity, it supposedly represents the egalitarian Australian ideal of giving everyone an equal turn. This has been interpreted in recent times as providing equality of opportunity, optimistically describing a former penal colony as the 'land of the fair go'. In practice, 'fair go!' is what people say when they want to whine about a perceived, potentially imaginary injustice.

— **'Fair go for those who have a go'** A phrase beloved of surprise and surprisingly enduring prime minister Scott Morrison, it means the exact opposite of the original 'fair go', suggesting that egalitarianism should be available only to a select few who have previously displayed entrepreneurial nous. Morrison has cited the owners of the undefeated racehorse Winx as an example of people deserving of a fair go because they had a go—apparently the government should render record-setting multimillionaires every assistance possible.

Fairlight CMI The Fairlight Computer Music Instrument was a hugely influential and groundbreaking digital synthesiser first launched in 1979—costing more than a house in Sydney at the time. It was one of the first products to allow digital sampling, and transformed popular music forever.

The Fairlight was used on countless 1980s pop songs including Frankie Goes To Hollywood's 'Relax', Tears For Fear's 'Relax', Kate Bush's 'Babooshka', and Yello's 'Oh Yeah'. It consequently has an awful lot to answer for.

The Fairlight was named after one of the Circular Quay to Manly hydrofoil ferries that regularly sailed past co-inventor Kim Ryrie's grandmother's harbourside house—the ferry itself was named after the Northern Beaches suburb. The Fairlight synth's technology is as outmoded nowadays as the hydrofoil ferry itself.

Fairy bread Sugared, food colouring–laced bread, served at children's parties to set the kids on a jolly path to diabetes. No fairies are involved in its production, but dentists are often involved in its aftermath.

Fat Cat and Friends The **Aldi** version of Here's Humphrey, this TV programme featured an anthropomorphic feline being fat-shamed for many years, without possessing the power of speech to respond.

Though cancelled in 1991 in most of the country, Fat Cat's Twitter account reveals that, astonishingly, he/it was still hosting telethons in Perth as recently as 2017, looking as young and corpulent as ever, which is to say, as dated as a children's television character developed in the early 1970s.

Fat Cat also had a decades-long tradition of saying goodnight to Perth's little boys and girls at 7.30 each night, which is why so many Western Australian children have developed night terrors.

Federal Police, Australian A national law enforcement organisation with special responsibility for national security, counter-terrorism and intimidating journalists. The AFP also provides policing in the ACT, which is a much larger task than it used to be now that the Territory has banned fireworks.

The AFP is a respected and trusted organisation, except by parents whose children are involved in smuggling drugs to Indonesia and risk the death penalty, or those accused of terrorism and subjected to arbitrary detention before the charges are dropped due to a lack of evidence, or whistleblowers revealing evidence of wrongdoing by the Australian government.

Peter Dutton is the minister who is irresponsible for the AFP.

Feral *Adj.* A domestic animal such as a cat that has gone wild.

Noun A wild human living outside the usual social controls of society, discernible by their scruffy clothing, florid scent, culturally appropriated dreadlocks and incessant bongo-playing. It sometimes pays to befriend ferals, as it can lead to a job as a staffer once they become Greens MPs.

First Australians A broad term understood as encompassing the many **Aboriginal and Torres Strait Islander** peoples who were the nation's original inhabitants, except by **Tony Abbott**, who takes it to mean the First Fleet.

FitzSimons, Peter A statuesque author and journalist whose massive stature is dwarfed only by the vast proportions of his books. In recent years the former Wallabies player has written so prolifically for the *Sydney Morning Herald*, at the same time as its print edition keeps shrinking, that he often seems to be its only writer. In his journalism career, FitzSimons mostly writes about rugby, why Sydney's stadiums should not be demolished, and why Sydney's rugby stadiums should not be demolished. In recent years he has written many powerful pieces about concussion in football, and wears a bright red warning bandana to warn others of the devastating effects of accidental head-butts.

Flannie/Flanno   The flannelette shirt is the height of **bogan** winter fashion, often worn unbuttoned around one's faded Billabong t-shirt. Popular retailers that stock flannies include Lowes, Kmart and Vinnies.

Flannies were highly fashionable in the 1990s, when they became associated with the grunge and slacker movement and its stars like Kurt Cobain, and even though they are no longer trendy, flannie wearers generally remain both grungy and slack.

Flick   1. A movie.

2. To 'give something the flick' is to get rid of it, or reject it. Sadly, Australian audiences tend to give Australian flicks the flick.

Flynn, Errol   The swashbuckling leading man was not only the forerunner of the current Australian invasion of Hollywood, but is the only Tasmanian renowned for the diversity of his sexual partners.

Flynn had a proclivity for young women, a house full of secret two-way mirrors and perhaps unsurprisingly, reportedly contracted an epic number of venereal diseases. He was especially known for playing Robin Hood, in an unusual take on the legendary bandit where he robbed from the rich and gave the poor venereal disease.

— **'In like Flynn'**   A phrase paying tribute to the speed of Errol Flynn's seduction skills, which supposedly led to his expulsion from Shore School in Sydney for getting dirty with a laundress—one of the first in a lifetime of such antics. Apparently he loved the phrase, and wanted to call his autobiography *In Like Me*.

Folau, Israel   A footballer with immense God-given talent whom the Lord chose to remove from professional sport by also giving him a burning desire to make homophobic posts on social media.

Fortitude Valley   An area of Brisbane known for its bustling, borderline **feral** bars and nightclubs. Its name derives from the recognition that a night out in Brisbane often requires genuine bravery—which is lacking in the city's cab drivers, who often refuse to stop for late-night passengers in 'the Valley'. In recent years, the area has become a tourist destination for Sydneysiders, who want to experience nightlife after 11pm.

Foxtel   Australia's monopoly pay television network, devoted to serving all Australians who haven't yet worked out how to use BitTorrent. In recent years, Foxtel has been strongly associated with *Game of Thrones*, both because it broadcasts the programme, and because winter is coming for its business model.

Fremantle doctor   A relieving sea breeze that makes being in Western Australia more pleasant than usual. Confusion about the meaning of this phrase may delay visitors to this coastal town who are attempting to find emergency health care.

Frydenberg, Josh   Will someday be the near-impossible answer to the trivia question 'Who was Scott Morrison's treasurer?'

Fuck me dead   An Australian expression of surprise that is never to be taken literally.

Funnel-web   An Australian spider of such aggression and toxic venom that nobody should ever visit **Sydney**, the city with the highest arachnid concentration. Their name derives from their habit of hiding in a burrow until a trip-wire tells them prey is near. They have benefited in recent years from the impact of Sydney's lockout laws, which have turned much of the city into a massive hole.

   An antivenom has successfully been introduced, but its continued production requires some people who spot funnel-webs to capture the spiders for milking, a task which can leave those who perform it in need of an antivenom.

Furphy   An exaggerated or erroneous story. This usage may derive from stories told around the water carts branded 'J Furphy and Sons' that were used in World War I, an early version of what later became known as 'water-cooler talk'. Although this theory is probably a furphy.

G

Gold Coast Combines the relaxation of a traditional Australian beach with the unpleasant alienation of a major city *(Chill Mimi)*

Gundagai The train has not run here for several decades due to an understandable lack of interest *(Matilda)*

G   The Melbourne Cricket Ground. The stadium's name was originally abbreviated to 'MCG', but AFL fans found that even saying those three letters consumed precious time that they preferred to spend shouting at the umpires for being blind.

Galah   1. A pink-breasted variety of cockatoo.
2. An idiot. It's unclear what the birds have done to deserve this, as cockatoos are quite intelligent for birds, and especially clever when it comes to stealing hot chips.

— **Flamin' galah**   Something only ever said by Alf Stewart from *Home and Away*, whenever his scriptwriters tire of 'flamin' mongrel' and 'flamin' yahoos'.

Gap year   An Australian tradition where, after the intense pressures of their final high school exams, leavers travel overseas for a year before taking on the far lesser pressures of university. Seeing as there are generally four months between the end of exams and the start of uni, and most 'gappers' spend their year away working in low-paid jobs to make ends meet, it's arguable which is the more pleasant option. But a gap year certainly allows new high school graduates to confront the brutal reality of the labour market for unskilled eighteen-year-olds in an interesting new location.

G'day A contraction of 'good day', used as a greeting, which dates back to at least the 1880s in Australia. The original, formal 'good day' is never used in Australia except by those playing butlers in school plays.

'G'day' is strongly associated with Paul Hogan thanks to a series of 1980s tourism advertisements that aired in America and elsewhere, and astonishingly haven't yet made the phrase go out of fashion. These were the same ads where he promised to 'put a shrimp on the barbie', despite that not being how we generally cook prawns, and nor even the word we use for them.

Geek 1. Someone who is academically or technically adept, yet socially awkward.

2. To look, as in 'have a geek at' something, which is generally as far as the other kind of geek gets romantically.

GetUp! A left-wing activist group that uses the internet to campaign for its members' beliefs, GetUp! has chalked up many policy victories, and also successfully convinced even its most ardent supporters that it should lose the **daggy** exclamation mark.

Otherwise, the group's most enduring achievement has been its decades-long campaign to convince its right-wing opponents to waste large amounts of time on fruitless inquiries into its legal status, as well as pouring large amounts of money on starting insipid 'right-wing GetUp!s', which fail to recognise that the majority of the

Coalition's ancient supporters don't know how to turn their computers on.

In 2019, one conservative group even appointed a 'hilarious' bogus GetUp! mascot, who rapidly disappeared from the national stage after he ill-advisedly posted a video of himself humping a poster of a female candidate. The group responsible, known as Advance Australia despite being obviously regressive, explained that they had recruited a backpacker from overseas to play 'Captain GetUp!', paying a high price for their support for casualisation.

Gilchrist, Adam   A former Australian wicketkeeper known primarily for his exciting onslaughts of slogging with the bat. Though off the ground he has a reputation as a nice guy with impeccable morals, he is not to be trusted because of his habit of 'walking'—that is, surrendering his wicket for the unacceptable reason that he knew that he was out, even if the umpires hadn't dismissed him.

This utterly un-Australian practice set 'Gilly' apart from the team, and rightfully so, because of the arrogance involved in denying his teammates the chance to cash in on an umpiring error. He probably wouldn't have gone along with that sandpaper plot, either.

Gillard, Julia   The first Australian female prime minister, Gillard never managed to transcend the brutal way in which she gained the job, despite saying 'moving forward' many thousands of times in an attempt to do so. With the benefit of hindsight, however, she now appears to have been ahead of her time in being underwhelmed by Kevin Rudd as PM. Regrettably for her, she failed to counter the subsequent trend of being underwhelmed by Julia Gillard as PM.

Gillard is now remembered by many as an efficient prime minister who not only passed a great deal of legislation but, more admirably still, efficiently disappeared when her colleagues dumped her, rather than wasting years trying to exact a futile, self-destructive revenge.

Gleeson, Tom A comedian who discovered that the secret to winning Gold Logies was to have utter contempt for the Logies. Having successfully campaigned for an ironic Gold Logie for Grant Denyer—despite the cancellation of his show—he went on to do the same for himself the following year.

It's unclear what Gleeson can possibly do to top this, rather like the proverbial dog that caught the car.

Glory box A receptacle where women store things for their future, hypothetical marriage. This use of the word 'glory' to describe married life no doubt originates from somebody who had never been married.

Godfreys A retailer specialising in vacuum cleaners that has been around since 1931, and is somehow still around even though every major retailer now sells vacuum cleaners, and Godfreys' only significant expansion since its foundation has been into steam mops.

Godfreys recently made the news after 99-year-old John Johnston, who first joined founder Godfrey Cohen as a partner in 1936, bought up the entire business. He died just months later, but is survived by more than 200 vacuum cleaner stores that surely won't still be around by 2036.

Gold Coast   While the Sunshine Coast reliably offers sunshine, visitors to Queensland's other famous beach strip should not make a similar assumption about anything valuable being on offer. The Gold Coast is, however, perfect for anyone who dislikes unspoilt beaches and prefers their seaside vistas crammed with the theoretical maximum of high-rise condos.

Goodes, Adam   One of the greatest Aussie rules players of all time, a dual premiership winner and Brownlow winner, as well as the Australian of the Year for 2014. However, Goodes ultimately found that none of his many accomplishments mattered to a large section of football fans who booed him for weeks and ultimately bullied him out of the game. This occurred after he took a strong stance against a racist taunt, even though his detractors convinced themselves they were only doing it because he allegedly 'milked free kicks', as opposed to their tall poppy syndrome, mob mentality and shitty, latent racism.

Goods and Services Tax (GST)   A 10 per cent impost on most goods and services except for food and certain other items considered essential, which were exempted after the Australian Democrats won these concessions in return for entirely destroying their political prospects. The GST was introduced by the Howard government in July 2000, replacing a host of state taxes, and the income it generates goes to the states to augment their favourite income source, gambling.

There was intense criticism of the tax before it was introduced due to its regressive nature, but after it arrived, most people promptly forgot about it. One controversial inclusion was tampons, which for some reason just possibly connected to the patriarchy, were not considered sufficiently essential to exempt from the GST until January 2019.

Some politicians have suggested that the GST is not high enough to be economically effective, and that it should be raised to 15 per cent. These people are immediately shouted down by the rest of their parties and forced to hide themselves away in a cupboard and/or think tank.

Goog   Being 'full as a goog' means drinking so much that you think you are like an egg. Being 'full as a goog' also frequently leads to being full of kebab.

Goon   Cheap wine from a cask. While the wine itself may be inexpensive, the experience of **sculling** goon at **Schoolies** and then **chundering** is a priceless rite of passage for young Australians.

— Goon bag   The foil bladder within a cardboard cask, which is often removed to faciliate the squirting of its contents into one's own mouth. Sadly, this Australian innovation has yet to catch on overseas, so our wine exports are generally shipped in inconveniently heavy glass bottles.

Gotye   The moniker of Wally de Backer, whose hugely successful musical project got the world singing his US number one and multiple Grammy-winning hit 'Somebody That I Used To Know' and wondering how on earth to pronounce 'Gotye'. Nowadays, eight years after his breakthrough album *Making Mirrors*, the world occasionally wonders whether he's going to release any more music, or just become somebody that we used to know.

Green ban   A stop-work order issued by a trade union or similar organisation to prevent property owners from demolishing a historically significant structure. As this cannot realistically be done without the assistance of experienced builders, green bans have been used to protect many buildings that are now regarded as historically significant. Builders have had less success in protecting their historic unions from embarrassing investigations.

Ironically, the notion of green bans has receded somewhat into history, as taking decisions on purely environmental grounds is not considered sensible in today's political climate, even as we rush headlong into a climate catastrophe.

Greens, Australian   A party formed to protect old-growth forests and armpits, the Greens blend sensible, pragmatic concern for the natural environment with fringe left-wing social policy. For much of their history, this has assisted them with alienating the mainstream from embracing their urgent, important environmental concerns.

On the rare occasions that the Greens have found themselves sharing the balance of power, they have tended to torpedo worthwhile incremental reform because it just isn't quiiiite 100 per cent perfect, you guys, sorry.

Nevertheless, the Greens have solidified their support base in recent years, and have remained the most electorally successful minor party for many years now. If nothing else, the Greens have succeeded in taking themselves off the endangered list.

Grey nomad   A well-known species within the dominant baby boomer genus, grey nomads are known for roaming far and wide across regional Australia, typically in caravans and motorhomes. They do this because evidently retirement is so boring that driving for hours across the flat, often tedious landscape of this enormous, largely uninhabited country is relatively entertaining.

Grey nomads are experts on Australia's famous **big things**, having visited all of them, and are also happy to explain in excessive detail which country towns have the best antique shops and bathroom facilities.

Gundagai   A NSW town famous for having a statue of a dog sitting on a tuckerbox five miles out of town, as per a popular song by Jack O'Hagan. This leads many overseas visitors to wonder just how low the bar for Australian tourist attractions really is, an impression that isn't improved on learning that it was unveiled by Prime Minister Joseph Lyons himself. Even O'Hagan himself never visited Gundagai until 44 years after releasing the song. It's not recorded whether he was underwhelmed after finally visiting the town he had made so famous.

Sadly, the statue was recently vandalised, leading to a proposal to install 24-hour CCTV in the area. Perhaps this will be streamed online so that the global audience that wishes to experience the majesty of a bronze dog sitting on a green box can do so without having to drive to Gundagai.

Gutful To have 'had a gutful' means being sick of something, and being unwilling to put up with any more of it. This phenomenon takes place especially rapidly during election campaigns.

— **Gutful of piss** Having consumed a large quantity of alcohol, so much that one forgets that urine accumulates in the bladder rather than the gut.

Guthrie, Michelle The first female managing director of the ABC, Guthrie was sacked by the board less than halfway through her five-year term due to concerns about her effectiveness. She refuted her critics by taking out the chairman who sacked her, **Justin Milne**, a mere three days later in a stunningly effective piece of upward feedback. Some ABC staff, however, wished Guthrie had been as successful in her efforts to rebuff the national broadcaster's external critics.

H

Hart, Pro A Rolls Royce that Hart ruined by painting on it *(Kr.afol)*

Holt, Harold Despite his tragic disappearance, Holt wasn't remembered fondly by everyone *(Beau Giles)*

Hadley, Ray A broadcaster who is renowned for his aggressive on-air style which, according to his former colleagues, is much gentler than his off-air style.

Previously a cab driver, Hadley has retained that profession's tendency to offer belligerent opinions on every topic, regardless of whether he has expertise in the area, and the success of his networked morning programme means that he can now be heard mouthing off in thousands of the nation's cabs instead of his previous role narrowcasting his rants to one passenger.

Hadley is also known for his work as the main presenter of the Continuous Call Team, a rugby league commentary team which operates across the weekend and is named in honour of Hadley's ability to speak non-stop for hours at a time.

Happy as Larry Exceptionally happy. The joyful Laurence whose delight gave rise to the expression is unknown, but it's simplest nowadays to think of it as meaning 'happy as Larry Emdur'.

Happy little Vegemite   A highly deceptive advertising campaign from the 1950s, as nobody whose diet consists of pungent yeast paste for breakfast, lunch and tea could possibly be happy or bright. The phrase has passed into more general, non-Vegemite-related usage, though nowadays is best only used sarcastically.

Hard yakka   1. Tough, demanding work, from 'yaga' in the Yagara language of the Brisbane region.
2. A relatively pricey brand of workwear, occasionally worn for tough, demanding work, but also often worn by people who wouldn't dream of doing anything so uncouth as physical labour.

Hart, Pro   A painter from Broken Hill, known for his exuberant paintings of outback life, and innovative methods of splattering paint onto his canvases. As he had no formal training, it's unclear why he called himself 'Pro'. Hart often used a cannon to shoot paint on the canvas, an approach which improved many of his artworks.

His best-known work was a dragonfly created on a large swatch of Dupont Stainmaster carpet using red wine, chocolate sauce and tinned spaghetti as well as paint, which he then crawled along. Tragically, it was erased by a cleaning lady shortly afterwards.

Hawke, Bob   A much-loved larrikin prime minister whose death caused a national outpouring of grief and fond remembrances by the Australian public, although not enough for them to vote Labor into office a few days later.

The many reflections on Hawke's career made it clear that no matter how much he accomplished in office—and his term as prime minister laid the foundations of modern Australia—he will always be most fondly remembered for his **beer sculling** record.

Healthy Harold   The mascot of Life Education, Healthy Harold visits kids in school to educate them about the dangers of drugs and alcohol—a brave choice, as excessive drug and alcohol consumption can sometimes create the illusion that animals are talking to you. Though the programme has been a success for 40 years, it's clear from the ongoing rates of drug and alcohol abuse that regrettably, not every Australian makes life decisions based on the advice of an anthropomorphic giraffe.

It's recently become clear that as well as visiting schools, Healthy Harold should start making educational visits to NRL clubs.

Hemsworth   A member of a superhuman tribe of Australian actor–surfers, known for their muscular physiques and chiselled good looks. Usually found in LA, Byron Bay, Asgard or Panem, Chris and Liam Hemsworth have appeared in some of the biggest movies of all time.

There is also an older, shorter brother, Luke, who was the only Hemsworth to receive formal training at NIDA. Evidently this only held him back from becoming an immediate Hemsworthian superstar. Even he is having success nowadays, however, with a major role in *Westworld*, because those Hemsworth supergenes will out.

Recently, Chris Hemsworth has come under fire because of his and his wife's construction of an enormous, boxy new home at **Byron Bay** costing $9 million, which unkind locals have likened to a **Westfield**. The project makes more sense when it's kept in mind that 95 per cent of the floorspace is a gym.

Henderson, Gerard Sydney Institute proprietor, media columnist and sometime dog impersonator, Henderson himself has a number of canine-like qualities, including difficulty letting go of things, extreme loyalty—in his case to the Catholic Church—and no discernible sense of humour. He is a major critic of the ABC, often for not inviting him to appear on the ABC as often as he would like.

Here's Humphrey A children's TV programme starring Humphrey B. Bear that was broadcast for many years on the Nine Network until producers realised it was unwise to teach kids to trust hairy male figures who don't wear pants.

Hi-vis Fluorescent workwear donned by workers who want to stand out from their environment for safety purposes. Also worn by politicians who want to blend in with working-class voters, yet cannot help but stand out even in a room full of other people wearing hi-vis.

High Court of Australia Australia's constitutional court, and final court of appeal. It had some big hits in the 1980s and 90s, such as the Tasmanian Dams, Chamberlain, **Mabo** and Wik decisions, and its landmark conclusion that Australia's Constitution implies certain rights. But though the court has continued to release new material each year, it has struggled to achieve much airplay since the era of these classic hits.

As with many courts, the judges are often perceived to be out of touch with ordinary Australian life—but in their defence, they are as in touch as it's possible to be when you've spent decades as successful lawyers, earn more than $500,000 per year, and work in a fancy lakeside building in Canberra.

The current chief justice, Susan Kiefel, is the first woman to hold the role, and as usual when a woman is appointed to a major position in public life for the first time in history, it's been absolutely fine, and nobody quite understands why it took so long. But given the gender balance issues across the judiciary, she will nevertheless probably be succeeded by another long series of men.

Hillsong   A Pentecostal or charismatic (or 'happy-clappy', an insulting if fairly accurate term) megachurch, or perhaps even gigachurch. It originated in Sydney's Bible Belt Hills District—hence the name Hillsong.

The church has gained worldwide recognition in Christian circles for its emotive, power ballad–style worship songs, which ultimately led to the church's leadership deciding to build on their brand recognition and change their organisation's name from the Hills Christian Life Centre to just 'Hillsong', much like the way Starbucks dropped the 'Coffee' from their name when people started coming in for Frappuccinos.

Hillsong is Australia's most successful home-grown religious organisation internationally, claiming to have 130,000 weekly worshippers around the world, and its success (and shortcomings) can be illustrated by Justin Bieber's enthusiastic attendance at their church.

Hillsong has more than 50 overseas branches in many of the world's biggest cities, and also, curiously, in Bali, where its pastors are known as the least drunk Australians on the entire island.

The church also has a 24/7 TV channel, a training college and a women's movement called the 'Colour Sisterhood', which is led by a white woman, rather awkwardly.

The praise anthems produced by the Hillsong machine are performed to thousands of people in huge annual conference events, during which attendees hold their arms up in the air as though they are serving as an antenna for the Holy Spirit, a gesture that weirded out many atheists when Scott Morrison did it during the election campaign, but presumably earned him enough Jesus midichlorian vibes to win the election.

Hillsong's albums feature heavily on the ARIA charts each year, and their offshoot rock band Hillsong United (helmed by the boss's son, much like Christianity itself) plays to stadiums in the United States, because Father God really loves hearing praise songs performed by a band that sounds like Coldplay with even less edge.

Hillsong is known for preaching a 'prosperity' gospel, where belief in God leads to material possessions in this life—just as Jesus was known for his healthy salary and habit of riding around on a motorbike, like Hillsong's Global Senior Pastor Brian Houston. The church is known for having ATMs, so its congregation can hand some of their God-fuelled financial bounty back to their church.

The original Christian Life Centre where Hillsong had its origins was founded by Brian's late father Frank Houston, who committed sexual assault against as many as nine boys—which led Brian (who was then the head not just of their church, but of the Assemblies of God congregations across Australia) to sack his father from the church he had founded, but not report the matter to the police. Brian was subsequently censured by the Royal Commission into Institutional Responses to Child Sexual Assault. This embarrassing criticism has apparently failed to put any kind of dampener on Hillsong's massive global expansion, perhaps because everyone was too busy singing joyful songs of praise to be concerned about the failure to report a serial paedophile.

Hobart   The capital of Tasmania, located on the southern coast of a small southern island facing Antarctica, and consequently just as freezing as that sounds. Hobart was the first European settlement outside NSW—colonial administrators soon got better at choosing city locations. The once-routinely overlooked city is now extremely popular with tourists, all of whom get straight on the ferry to **MONA**.

Holey dollar   The first currency issued by the colony of New South Wales, it was produced by punching holes in Spanish doubloons, providing a doughnut-shaped coin worth five shillings, as well as the 'dump', which was made from the central punched-out portion, which was valued at 15p. The coin was the forerunner of the modern Australian dollar, which also frequently has large chunks taken out of its value.

The holey dollar later inspired the doughnut-shaped logo of Macquarie Bank, which owes part of its great success to its tendency to gouge out money via hefty management fees.

Holt, Harold To 'do a Harold Holt', or just a 'Harold' or 'Harry', is to disappear. Some have suggested that this is an example of rhyming slang, the rhyming word that provides the meaning being 'bolt', but the circumstances of former prime minister Holt's mysterious disappearance surely fit just as well without the need for any rhyme.

It's worth clarifying the phrase is only used when somebody has rapidly and unexpectedly departed, much like the practice of sudden departure known as 'ghosting' nowadays. It is unknown whether Holt himself is also a ghost.

'Doing a Harry' does not mean 'drowning on a beach', or 'escaping into a Chinese mini-submarine', or even 'having a public swimming pool in Melbourne ironically named after you'.

Honey badger This fiercely defensive creature has provided a nickname to both the moustachioed rugby star Nick Cummins and the refreshingly clean-shaven motor racing star Daniel Ricciardo. They really should have fought, honey badger style, over who gets the nickname, but true to type, neither is willing to concede anything.

Cummins was the star of a pointless series of *The Bachelor*, which culminated in him choosing not to pair off with any contestant—another thing he's very defensive about. Hiring him in the first place was arguably unwise, as honey badgers are known for living solo in holes in the ground.

Hoon An idiot who drives dangerously. Lexicographers are unclear about its origins, as it seems to have just appeared in the vocabulary of Australians, much like a hoon fanging down the road before doing a burnout in his hotted-up V8.

Hooroo Goodbye. This expression has been used for many years as a sign-off by Don Burke on *Burke's Backyard*—although his recent reputational challenges may have helped Australians say hooroo to 'hooroo'.

Though a little quaint nowadays, it must be conceded that 'hooroo' is considerably better than Rex Hunt's *Looney Tunes*-inspired sign-off 'it's yibbida yibbida time'.

House of Representatives In the Westminster tradition, the Federal Lower House's 151 members are chosen on the basis of geography, with each electorate carefully weighted to represent an approximately equal number of people. This system is designed to allow elected representatives to cast their votes in accordance with the wishes of the communities they represent.

In practice, they don't, and voters are generally forced to choose between members of the two major parties who are able to form government, who will almost always follow party lines regardless of how legislation would affect their specific electorates. The alternative is to opt for a wild card minor party member, or an independent MP, both of which options can only really be effective if there's a hung parliament.

Increasing numbers of Australian voters have become disillusioned with the system, as it provides only a choice between two thoroughly uninspiring prime ministers.

It's not surprising that the Westminster system is unsat-
isfactory, as even the most casual observer of the UK
parliament in recent years will have realised that the
original Westminster House of Commons that inspired
our lower house has ended up a roiling mess of contradic-
tions and egomania that has become incapable of making
decisions.

How good! The highest form of praise possible in
contemporary Australia, 'How good!' has been enthusiastically adopted by prime minister **Scott Morrison**
as part of his campaign to sound like an ordinary bloke, as
opposed to the kind of guy who's into giving hefty tax cuts
to millionaires.

The phrase can be used to praise a specific thing, as
in 'How good is Australia!', or can just be given as a non-
specific exhortation, as in 'How good!' It's phrased as a
question, but because of the overwhelming **dinkumness**
of its subject, it requires no answer.

Humphries, Barry A legendary actor and performer
who has spent much of his career taking an exaggerated
version of his own conservative Melbourne mother to
the world stage, questioning the notion that imitation is the
sincerest form of flattery.

Humphries is also known for playing the debauched
politician Sir Les Patterson, a character that has seemed
much less of a comic exaggeration with the rise to prominence of **Barnaby Joyce**.

INXS Lead singer Michael Hutchence's sex appeal was an unstoppable force, except in this photo (*David.moreno72*)

It's A Royal Knockout When the royal family watched the spectacular *It's A Knockout*, they wanted to be part of it (*Channel Ten via NFSA*)

'I Am Australian'   A patriotic song that many Australians would prefer as our national anthem. In its favour, it acknowledges the diversity of modern Australia and is harmlessly uplifting; against it is that it was recorded by The Seekers and was used in an ad for Telstra.

INXS   A brilliant pop-rock band that conquered the world in the 1980s and 90s, in particular with their smash album hit *Kick*. The group's appeal relied heavily on their handsome, charismatic singer Michael Hutchence, who was irreplaceable, as the band took several decades to realise after his sudden death in 1997.

It's A Knockout   The greatest show in the history of Australian television, *It's A Knockout* pitted four teams against one another in a series of absurd challenges where they got knocked into swimming pools with various large foam objects. It was somewhat like *Gladiators* and *Ninja Warrior*, but much better.

The show was discontinued in 1987 due to noise complaints from thoroughly un-Australian residents in

Dural where the show was filmed, all of whom should have been dunked repeatedly in the *Knockout* pool and bludgeoned with giant foam objects for their insolence.

An attempt to bring it back in 2011 failed because nobody could recapture the perfection of the original production. Curiously, it was filmed in Malaysia, the Dural of the Pacific.

— *It's A Royal Knockout*   Formally known as *The Grand Knockout Tournament*, the programme was the major venture of Prince Edward's brief yet glorious career as a television producer. Though a British production, it can be considered Australian due to the involvement of our beloved royal family.

Teams raised money for charity, and were captained by Princes Edward and Andrew, along with Princesses Anne and the Duchess of York, Sarah 'Fergie' Ferguson. The huge list of A-grade celebrity contestants willing to humiliate themselves on prime time television in return for an association with the royals included Christopher Reeve, John Cleese, Tom Jones, Sunil Gavaskar, Kevin Kline, Cliff Richard, Jane Seymour, John Travolta, Margot Kidder, Meat Loaf, Michael Palin, and perhaps most curiously of all, opera singer Dame Kiri Te Kanawa.

The show was considered a failure even though in one round the contestants dressed as giant chess pieces, and in another they dressed as giant vegetables and threw fake hams at each other.

The Queen had disapproved of the idea and advised Prince Edward against it. She was correct—it was highly tacky for the royal family to try and burnish their reputations via an association with the legendary *It's A Knockout*.

Jackman, Hugh His *X-Men* performance was compelling—and when not shredding punks with his adamantium claws, he's also a charming song-and-dance man *(20th Century Fox)*

Joyce, Barnaby Visiting a fruit company as Deputy PM, before everything went pear-shaped *(Apple and Pear Australia Ltd)*

J-curve   Used by **Paul Keating** to illustrate why the 'recession we had to have' would ultimately lead to future prosperity, the J-shaped graph instead modelled the Coalition vote leading up to the 1996 election.

Jacenko, Roxy   As a member of the Australian media, the author is obliged to include a breathless, unnecessary mention of this publicist to the stars—who is a star influencer herself these days! Hi Roxy, if you're reading this—can you Instagram about the book? Thanks in advance xox.

Jackaroo   1. A young male worker on an outback cattle or sheep station, in many cases seeking experience as a form of apprentice. The female version, 'Jillaroo', emerged during the WWII, when women were required to perform many roles traditionally held by men, even jobs which were well known to be poorly paid, as those performing them were said to receive valuable experience. This was a forerunner of current internet employment practices where young workers are expected to work for free for 'exposure'.

2. A mid-sized four-wheel drive produced by Holden. Despite the distinctively Australian name, these cars were manufactured by Isuzu in Japan, just as Holden itself is as authentically Australian as a wholly owned subsidiary of Detroit's General Motors can be.

Jackman, Hugh   An Australian actor, singer and cabaret star who has become legendary for playing *X-Men* tough guy the Wolverine. He portrayed the adamantine-clawed mutant on the big screen for 18 years, building his muscle mass up to absurd proportions each time, while also simultaneously being a razzle-dazzle song-and-dance man who spent many years playing Peter Allen in *The Boy From Oz* and recently delighted audiences as P.T. Barnum in *The Greatest Showman*. Surprisingly, Jackman has yet to combine his best-known roles, and appear in a Wolverine musical.

Jackman is one of the very few Hollywood stars about whom absolutely nobody ever says a bad word, and seems like one of the nicest people on the planet despite his extraordinary success, meaning that he is probably hiding some absolutely abominable secrets.

Joyce, Barnaby   A former deputy prime minister and Nationals leader whose main achievements in recent years have been undermining his prime minister by foisting unpopular hard right policies on him, and undermining his own marriage by fathering a child with a staffer. Joyce retains his staunch opposition to same-sex marriage, as he believes people should only cheat on spouses of the opposite sex.

Jumbuck   A word for 'sheep' that Banjo Paterson clearly just made up.

K

Kings Cross   The 'Cross' back in the good old bad old days *(Sardaka)*

Kyrgios, Nick   A rare photo of Kyrgios trying *(Carine06)*

Kangaroo Referring to a large macropod, 'kangaroo' is the first and probably best-known word appropriated into English from an Aboriginal language. Joseph Banks initially recorded the word (as 'kanguru', which did not catch on) during Cook's 1770 expedition, taking it from the Guugu Yimidhirr language of North Queensland, just as a few years later the First Fleet would go on to take the entire country.

The kangaroo was so different from any European animal that the animal became a sensation in the UK, meaning that when the First Fleet arrived, they were already using the word. This confused the Eora people, who spoke a totally different language, and called them 'patagaram'. Had Banks not managed to record the word, it's possible that we would be ordering our meals from Delivergaram instead of Deliveroo.

— **Kangaroo court** A dodgy court with no legal standing, such as a Logies jury.

— **Kangaroo route** The route flown between the UK and Australia via Asia, most commonly used to refer to the route between Sydney and London which Qantas flies as QF1. That kangaroo-logoed airline has trademarked the term, and originated the service, which is now flown by other, better airlines as well.

Following its Emirates partnership, Qantas started to stop over in Dubai, but by 2018 it was back to using Singapore as it had since the earliest days of the route. This was due to passenger demand, probably because it's a lot easier to go out drinking in Singapore.

In 1947, it took 77 hours to get from Sydney to London. By 2022, Qantas plans to fly directly between the two cities, which would be the world's longest passenger flight. That journey would take just 20 hours, but feel like 77 to anyone doing it in economy.

— **Kangaroos loose in the top paddock**   Crazy. As a farming-based metaphor, it's particularly appropriate for eccentric politicians representing a rural constituency, such as **Barnaby Joyce** or **Bob Katter**.

Katter, Bob   A conservative politician from North Queensland, Katter is known for his large shock of white hair, his even larger hat, and idiosyncratic speech patterns that can only be simulated by feeding a dictionary into a combine harvester, and then tossing the resulting fragments into a tropical cyclone.

Katter is, however, entirely intelligible to the people of North Queensland, who consider him a straight-talking fount of common sense. It should be noted, though, that like Katter, their brains have also been affected by prolonged exposure to tropical heat.

Keating, Paul Renowned as a polymath, public intellectual and accomplished insult comic, Keating would have been prime minister for more than four years if our barbaric system did not require the leader of the day to submit himself to the indignity of elections. Pshaw!

Outside of politics, Keating is renowned as a collector of French Empire clocks, recordings of Gustav Mahler and grudges.

Kenny, Chris Media commentator who frequently accuses people to his left of 'virtue signalling', a term he employs to prove his ideological virtue to those on the right, along with his employers at *The Australian* and Sky News.

Chris Kenny's other perpetual theme is criticising the ABC for not employing enough people like Chris Kenny. He is fond of satirising the national broadcaster's long-time slogan 'our ABC' as 'their ABC', even though he seems to consume its broadcasts more than just about anybody.

Kerr, Sir John Former Governor-General who somehow decided that his role representing the Queen, who meticulously respects the long-standing tradition that a monarch doesn't interfere in politics, required him to collude with the Opposition to sack the elected government of the day.

Gough Whitlam described Malcolm Fraser, the man who would replace him, as 'Kerr's cur', a clever bit of wordplay that no doubt made him feel better, but did not otherwise help his situation.

'Khe Sanh' Cold Chisel song and strong contender to become the national anthem, dealing as it does with such contemporary Australian themes as the cloying dullness of suburbia, fly-in fly-out mining jobs, self-medication with illicit drugs, messy visits to Asia, and the lasting impacts of trauma caused by being dragged into wars that have little to do with Australia.

Another strong argument in its favour is that it does not contain the word 'girt'.

Kings Cross   A quiet inner-Sydney suburb once known for sex, drugs and bohemian counterculture. There is no longer any reason to visit, but students of urban decay occasionally wander down the once-notorious Golden Mile to marvel at the boarded-up nightclubs and strip clubs, along with property developers planning the demolition of once-famous heritage venues for another giant block of generic apartments.

'The Cross' has, however, retained its safe injecting room, a rare triumph of rationality over cheap moralising in Australian drugs policy, which has been credited with saving many lives. The injecting room's presence in what is nowadays a ghost town means that the few non-residents who now wander through the deserted streets of Kings Cross are junkies on their way to shoot up, which gives residents of the area's many fancy new apartment buildings an occasional taste of the decadent Cross their lifestyle helped to destroy.

Knights and Dames   Following on from the Order of Australia's introduction under Gough Whitlam's Labor government, which ended the imperial honours system in Australia, the ranks of Knight (AK) and Dame (AD) of the Order of Australia were introduced by Liberal PM Malcolm Fraser in 1976.

Bob Hawke of Labor abolished knights and dames again in 1983, and then **Tony Abbott** of the Liberal Party brought them back in 2014.

The decision to award Prince Philip an Australian knighthood was widely ridiculed, although it should be noted that his lucky son Prince Charles had already been given one—the fact that almost nobody was aware of this just shows how prestigious the award was.

The cycle was broken when **Malcolm Turnbull** decided to revoke knight and dame awards despite being a Liberal, which only furthered suspicions by many on the right that he was at heart something of a Labor man.

Koch, David 'Kochie'   A veteran finance journalist who used his business expertise to spot a gap in the market and rebrand himself as an unlikely breakfast television everyman. He even managed to sell a successful series of 'Kochie's Best Jokes' books despite being the furthest thing imaginable from a comedian. But his buttoned-down persona remains popular with viewers who want nothing more than to eat breakfast with an affable headmaster.

Kochie's success in retaining his *Sunrise* chair when his bosses dumped his original co-host Melissa Doyle for the younger Sam Armytage didn't reflect any particular nous on his part, however—it's just what happens to women on Australian television.

Kyrgios, Nick Australian tennis player who has shown regular flashes of brilliance and beaten several of the world's top players, but has not experienced sustained success due to his inability to overcome his own lack of interest. Nevertheless, Kyrgios has won widespread recognition for his consistent innovation in the areas of abusive language, serving underarm and deliberately losing matches in tournaments when he'd rather be doing something else.

Lamington As Australian as pavlova, or as New Zealander *(Bidgee)*

Laneway An ordinary, unremarkable laneway in Melbourne *(Bernard Spragg)*

Labor Party   The main left-wing party in Australia, Labor is the one place in Australian society where trade unions still have significant influence. The party's natural affinity with the overwhelming majority of citizens who make up Australia's labour force has, surprisingly, led to Labor struggling to win national elections, as aspirational voters tend to vote against their class interests by falsely convincing themselves that they're a few paydays away from joining the wealthy elite.

As has been the case with many socialist movements the world over, many Labor politicians have frequently been part of the wealthy elite the party supposedly opposes, thanks to either a privileged background or epic corruption.

Lairy   A fancypants mode of dress designed to make the wearer seem impressive—generally a taboo in Australian society. It's been widely observed that Melburnian men are less concerned about appearing lairy than most Australians. After all, if everybody in a city dons a jaunty British peacoat, or sports a pair of terribly spiffing suspenders, none of them can be criticised for their lairiness.

Lamington A cube of sponge cake covered in chocolate icing and sprinkles of desiccated coconut, the lammo (Wikipedia says they're known by this nickname, and if that's incorrect, they nevertheless should be) is yet another legendary Australian foodstuff that New Zealand outrageously claims to have invented first, just because it may well have.

One theory is that the name derives from Baron Lamington, the governor of Queensland in Victorian times. There's a story that his French chef catered to last-minute guests by dipping left-over sponge cake in chocolate and coconut, which proved an unexpected hit with his guests. Another theory is that the Baron was known for prolific dandruff, although this theory was invented by the author.

Some early New Zealand recipes are spelt 'lemmington', which both challenges this derivation and evokes the image of pastries throwing themselves off a cliff.

In 2009, as part of the celebration of the 150th anniversary of the foundation of the state of Queensland, the lamington was celebrated as one of the icons of the style and hailed as an 'invention that Queenslanders have pioneered' alongside the Weis bar and Lucas' Pawpaw Ointment, making for a depressing portrait of the collective ingenuity of Queenslanders.

Laneway 1. The most important thoroughfares in Melbourne, with a direct correlation between how obscure, inaccessible and rat-infested a laneway is and how cool it is considered to be by the local fashionistas.

Melbourne's council also has a habit of renaming its laneways to honour local luminaries, meaning that the maps to the city's coolest places are often out of date. Given Melbourne's love of exclusivity, it's quite possible that the city contains secret laneways that aren't on any maps, and can only be accessed Diagon Alley-style, by pressing one's waxed moustache into the side of an overflowing dumpster.

Melbourne reached an unsurpassable peak of irritating laneway coolness in 2006, when the then impossibly trendy folk band Bon Iver debuted their trendily titled album *22, A Million* in a Fitzroy laneway. Local hipsters gathered to listen to a recording of the new album played from a boombox on cassette tape. And while this may sound like an absurdly comic exaggeration of Melburnity, it cannot be emphasised enough that this is a thing that actually happened.

Ironically, the city's designers intended Melbourne to be renowned for its wide boulevards.

2. A music festival originally known as the St Jerome's Laneway Festival, which originated in Melbourne's tiny Caledonian Lane. None of the festival's other venues across the country are in laneways, because only Melburnians would think it was a great idea to hold a gathering of thousands of people in an extremely cramped space.

Larrikin The major component of Australia's self-image, a larrikin is an easygoing type who loves a laugh and takes nothing seriously, not even themself. Of course, the reality for most Australians is stressed-out exhaustion due to our relatively long working hours, unaffordably high cost of living and general insecurity due to our remoteness from the rest of the world, which leads many Australians to suspect they may be living in a backwater, but never dare to admit this publicly. Still, everyone loves a larrikin!

Latham, Mark　A politician, media commentator and personality disorder case study. Latham is most notable for his anger, one of Australia's most abundant natural resources, which he has recently learned to tap to generate political power. Latham has undertaken a long, slow journey from the Labor leadership to the political far right, and a parallel journey from the front page of every newspaper to obscure Facebook live broadcasts.

Recently, however, Latham succeeded in returning to prominence after being elected as a One Nation upper house MP in NSW. He cannot be sacked from this position for making offensive statements—as he was by several media proprietors—until voters go to the polls in eight years. He will soon leave One Nation because they're a bunch of bleeding heart lefties.

Latham is known for despising 'elites', while also writing a cookbook with his good mate and political donor Alan Jones. He once broke a cabbie's arm after a dispute over a fare, because that's something a stable human with no anger management issues would definitely do.

Launceston　Tasmania's second largest city has a mere 84,000 residents, and largely exists so people from **Hobart** (230,000 residents) can feel like they inhabit a bustling metropolis by comparison.

Launceston is in the north of Tasmania, and consequently a surprisingly long drive from Hobart. In recent years, Hobart's Museum of Old and New Art (**MONA**) has relocated its summer MONA FOMA festival to Launceston, to test whether their events really can draw a crowd anywhere. Turns out they can.

Legless   1. So drunk that someone temporarily loses the use of their limbs.

2. Australian pronunciation of that elf from *Lord of the Rings*.

3. Not having a leg to stand on, which is what the author will have if asked to defend the inclusion of definition #2.

Liberal Party   Unlike most other countries where the term means 'progressive', the Liberals are the main Australian conservative party, thanks to an elaborate joke by its founder, noted humorist Sir Robert Menzies.

It usually operates in coalition with the National Party, which, equally absurdly, is strictly regional in its scope. Their coalition has worked, however, because regional and rural voters despise city slickers, and Nats are very good at lobbying for farm subsidies.

Light on the hill   Ben Chifley's famous summary of Labor's drive for social justice, which he described as 'the light on the hill, which we aim to reach by working for the betterment of mankind'. In the years since his famous 1949 speech, however, Australians have more often than not interpreted this light as a red warning beacon.

Lilley, Chris   Comic actor known for his chameleon-like ability to transform from a white guy into a white guy in drag and/or blackface.

Longneck   A superior design of beer bottle, in that it holds twice as much. In reality, the neck is virtually the same length as the top of a **stubby**, but 'longbody' would have sounded peculiar.

Lucky Country   A complimentary nickname for Australia. Ironically, it was initially used in a negative sense by the author Donald Horne in his book of the same name—he was warning against complacency, since in his words, 'Australia is run by second-rate people who share its luck'. He thought that as a result we should not take our natural resources for granted but instead focus on becoming a cleverer, more enterprising country.

However, due to the anti-intellectualism Horne diagnosed, most Australians didn't bother to engage with Horne's argument, instead assuming it was meant as a compliment.

M

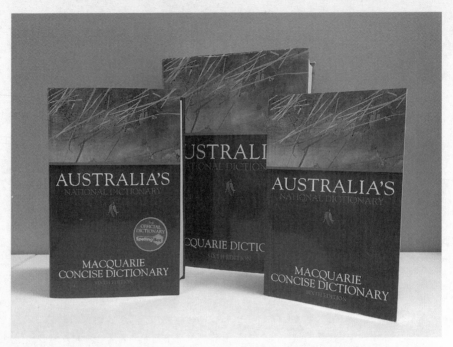

Macquarie Dictionary Now the second most reputable Australian dictionary *(Br8so)*

Megafauna The skeleton of a carnivorous goanna that grew up to 7 metres long and could have devoured the entire band Goanna

Mabo A landmark 1992 **High Court** decision which established that some native title could have survived the British Crown's ~~theft~~ settlement of the vast majority of Australian land, overturning the application of the doctrine of terra nullius in strictly limited cases. Even though it was restricted to land over which nobody else had ever been given title, this proved to be enough to make the usual suspects go absolutely apeshit about the impossible prospect of Indigenous Australians claiming their backyard swimming pools and pergolas.

Eddie Mabo launched the case on behalf of the Meriam people of the Torres Strait, but died a few months before the fundamental justice of his claim was recognised by the court. His original grave site was later vandalised by racists who painted swastikas and the word 'Abo' on it, because Straya. But he was ultimately reburied on his ancestral island of Mer, and given a traditional king's funeral, because of course.

Macca's A once enjoyable Australian nickname for McDonald's, it has stopped being fun since the company leaned into it and trademarked the nickname. It went on to release such anodyne initiatives as 'mymacca's', of which it says 'mymacca's is your Macca's®. An experience where you're at the heart of everything. You're an Insider who gets the inside scoop of everything Macca's'.

This is a huge claim when 'everything Macca's' just means burgers and fries.

Macquarie Dictionary Australia's national dictionary from 1981 until the publication of this one.

Macropods A marsupial family that includes kangaroos, wallabies, **pademelons**, bettongs and other creatures routinely shamed by biologists for their enormous feet.

Mad as a cut snake Very mad. It's not known who first cut a snake to test this, but there should be no debate that a cut snake would be madder than an intact one.

Mad as a meataxe Also very mad. This phrase is confusing, as the danger is surely from a mad person wielding a meataxe, rather than the meataxe itself.

Made in Melbourne A phrase that parochial Melburnians enjoy seeing written on the side of trams, or placed in the local ad breaks of locally made programmes which go to national audiences, with the slogan not broadcast outside that city. Sydney programmes never say 'Made in Sydney', both because Sydneysiders don't really care that much and because most programmes are. Other cities don't boast about their locally made programmes because they don't have any.

Magic Pudding, The Norman Lindsay's prescient 1918 tale of a 'cut-an-come-again' pudding that regenerated no matter how many slices were cut from it taught generations of Australians that there was no need to prepare for future austerity, an approach that still bedevils Australian economic planners today. The fixation on consuming puddin' also foreshadowed Australia's obesity crisis.

A modern version of *The Magic Pudding* would tell the story of an irascible credit card that pays itself off as soon as you use it.

Magnetic Island A small island off the coast of Townsville that got its name because Captain James Cook thought, incorrectly, that it contained iron deposits in its hills that were interfering with his compass.

The author once spent an afternoon wandering around the island hoping to observe its mysterious magnetic effect on his phone compass, and will never make that mistake again.

Mallee bull 'As fit as a Mallee bull' is a simile referring to a bull strong enough to fight through scrubland. Increasingly, however, the appropriate bovine metaphor for Australians is as 'fat as a fattened calf'.

Manchester A term for household linen, which was traditionally manufactured at the cotton mills there. It's unclear why Australians ever wanted anything in their bedrooms that was associated with this dreary English city.

Maralinga The traditional home of the Maralinga Tjarutja people, this area in the west of South Australia was considered sufficiently uninhabited for Britain to conduct seven nuclear tests there in the 1950s. But as usual, the British were far from skilled at determining whether Australia was uninhabited, and many of the local Aboriginal people went on to accuse the British of giving them radiation-related illnesses. There are also many claims of premature deaths.

The local Aboriginal people were eventually paid substantial compensation and given title to their traditional land, which admittedly was not in huge demand for agriculture, what with it still being radioactive.

British and Australian soldiers were deliberately exposed to radiation at Maralinga to assess its impacts, many without protective clothing. Unastoundingly, the impacts were fairly devastating—many of those affected died younger than they should have, often of radiation-related diseases. Some maintain that the exposure produced severe, sometimes fatal illnesses in their offspring as well.

All in all, the tests were a low point in Britain's relationship with Australia, lying somewhere on the colonial heinousness scale in between sending us John Farnham and grabbing the entire continent to begin with.

Mardi Gras The Sydney Gay and Lesbian Mardi Gras is a pride march that had its origin in a 1978 protest that led to a brutal police backlash and the incarceration of several of those involved. The annual parade down Oxford St became gradually more accepted over time, however, especially as the surrounding suburb of Darlinghurst transitioned into a gay and gay-friendly district. Eventually, the Mardi Gras parade became a tourist drawcard, and so popular with the people of NSW that large companies now use it to make their brands seem progressive.

Nowadays the NSW Police even have their own float in the parade, after which none of the officers involved have ever felt the need to beat or arrest themselves.

These decades of steady progress have been entirely lost on a small core of hardcore Christian Mardi Gras opponents such as the Reverend Fred Nile. His annual prayers for rain are generally ignored by the Almighty, in keeping with the Bible's clear view that 'God is Love', and Jesus' obvious preference for hanging out with those shunned by his society's powerful religious leaders.

Mate   A word that Australians believe to be uniquely Australian, even though it's also widely used in England with its original meaning of a friend.

In modern Australia, however, it's used to refer to someone that the speaker likes, or dislikes, or whose name they can't remember, and therefore it explains nothing about the relationship involved.

The word has traditionally had male-only overtones, rather ironically given the other meaning of mate, as in a romantic life partner with whom one can procreate.

— **Mateship**   The supposed touchstone among Australian cultural values where people (traditionally men, if we're honest) from all walks of life band together against a common enemy. The term is mostly used nowadays by politicians who are trying to demonise their opponents or just generally be patronising.

Matilda   1. A swagman's name for their swag, as in 'Waltzing Matilda'. The ANU's *Ozwords* has suggested that 'Matilda' in this context has its origin in the nickname of German sex workers who accompanied that country's soldiers into war—without one of them, a swagman was reduced to cuddling up with his swag, which was given the joking nickname of Matilda as well. The ANU has also suggested that 'waltzing' referred to rolling up the swag (*walzen* in German), rather than dancing in 3/4 time with it, which makes considerably more sense.

2. A member of the excellent Australian women's football team, known as the Matildas and named after the song. This nickname seems significantly less charming if the derivation described above is to be believed.

McGuire, Eddie   A feudal warlord who has the entire city of Melbourne under his undisputed control, leading him to earn the nickname 'Eddie Everywhere'—although this is somewhat misleading, as his ubiquity is limited to the immediate inner city.

McGuire's long-term presidency of the Collingwood Football Club guarantees his popularity with supporters of the AFL's powerhouse club, and it's a testament to his absolute dominance that supporters of the clubs that despise Collingwood—that is, all the other clubs—continue to consume his radio and TV shows nevertheless.

McGuire has successfully maintained his power base for several decades despite regular scandals when he speaks his mind a little too freely. He even survived a brief period as CEO of the Nine Network, which led him to conclude that he should never take another job where he's required to travel outside of Melbourne.

McOz   A **Macca's** burger launched in 1999 that contained **beetroot** along with salad, cheese and ketchup. Arguably the most Australian thing about it is that a similar burger was also sold in New Zealand as the Kiwiburger, which would have led to the usual arguments over its origins had either survived for long on the menu. Disappointingly, the Kiwiburger also contained an egg, which really should have been in the McOz as well, along with pineapple.

Despite the McOz being designed to replicate a traditional Australian burger, its disappearance suggests either that Australians don't actually like beetroot on their burgers, or the McDonald's version was not great. The author suspects both may be true.

Medicare   Australia's universal healthcare system, first introduced under Gough Whitlam as Medibank, effectively taken away by Malcolm Fraser as he introduced Medibank Private, and then brought back by Bob Hawke under the current friendlier name. Subsequently, John Howard boosted the private health sector but left Medicare as the universal safety net, as the notion that every Australian should be entitled to healthcare is now effectively politically untouchable, no matter how many times the idea of co-payments is floated and then abandoned.

Medicare guarantees every Australian access to lifesaving treatment when they urgently need it—and for the rest of the time, there's always queueing.

Megafauna   Though the term refers simply to large animals, and some creatures that still exist like the red kangaroo qualify under biologists' current definition, the most interesting megafauna are the enormous ones that once roamed Australia. This country was once home to a sheep-sized variety of echidna, a 3 metre high kangaroo species, and the diprotodon, a wombat-like creature the size of a minibus and much harder to drive.

There were also leopard-sized marsupial lions, huge platypuses and a 2.5 metre long creature somewhat like a tapir, which devoured trees, stripping the bark. There was also the Demon Duck of Doom, or *mihirung*, a native bird that got up to 2.5 metres high and 300 kilograms in weight. Though its wings were tiny and useless, it could run very quickly, making it the most terrifying duck-like creature seen in Australia until the advent of *Hey Hey It's Saturday*'s Plucka Duck.

The extraordinary array of enormous megafauna that has been discovered in Australia's fossil record leads to an obvious question—who will use DNA records to reconstruct these creatures as the centrepieces of Australia's very own Jurozic Park? Anyone with the geneticist know-how or who has the limitless funds required should contact the author at dominic.knight@gmail.com using the subject line 'Jurozic Park'. Clive Palmer need not apply, as he cannot be trusted when it comes to animatronic dinosaur parks, let alone the real deal.

Melba   To 'do a Melba' is to make repeated comebacks, as the opera singer Dame Nellie Melba did. Given the controversy (and amusement) surrounding his 2002–3 *Last Time* tour, which has been followed by multiple subsequent tours, the phrase should probably be updated to 'doing a Farnham'.

Meter Maids   A programme that has existed since 1965, when local Gold Coast businesses decided to undermine the council's decision to install parking meters to guarantee their customers parking spots by paying bikini-clad women to roam around Surfers Paradise, feeding expired meters. This bizarre project is often described as an 'institution' nowadays, which provides the tiniest fig leaf to justify not abandoning an obvious anachronism. And yet they really, really should.

Migration zone   The area where Australia's Migration Act is considered to operate. Originally this was anywhere within Australian territory, but applying Australian law consistently throughout Australia soon came to seem problematic because it required the government to be more considerate than it wanted to be.

At first the Howard government excised outlying islands like **Christmas Island** so that asylum seekers couldn't land there and remain in Australia while their claims were processed, and this policy proved such an effective deterrent to desperate people looking to make a better life in Australia that the Gillard government decided to excise the whole of the Australian mainland.

Consequently, for the purposes of the international asylum system, where anyone arriving in a place has traditionally had the right to stay while their claim is processed, there is no such thing as Australia. That said, Australia is still the best legally non-existent country in the world.

Milk bar   A traditional neighbourhood fast food joint whose menu is far broader than the name implies, but calls itself a 'milk bar' because milk is the only thing on sale that's guaranteed to be healthy. The exception to this is when it's made into milkshakes, which are always sold in large metal containers that freeze the hands of the customer.

Milk bars generally sell burgers (with **beetroot**), chips, spring rolls, **Chiko rolls**, Dagwood dogs, kranskys, potato **scallops** and anything else that can be purchased frozen and placed in the deep fryer. They also sell ice creams and newspapers, although these are disappearing even more rapidly than milk bars.

Milne, Justin   Former ABC chairman appointed by then-prime minister Malcolm Turnbull, his good mate and former colleague at OzEmail. Astonishingly, Milne was subsequently accused of trying to limit ABC independence by dumping presenters Emma Alberici and Andrew Probyn because of concerns that the government would object to their reporting, as well as interfering with triple j and the comedy show *Tonightly* for similar reasons. Milne denies this, and says his emails were taken 'out of context', an excuse which admittedly makes him seem like an ideal person to handle governmental relations in 2019.

Mining   A terrific industry that generates much revenue and many jobs for ordinary Australians, is absolutely above reproach environmentally, especially given the evolution of wonderful modern techniques like 'clean coal', leaves no lasting damage even when a project happens near the Great Barrier Reef, and definitely does not need to give any more of its income to taxpayers in the form of a super profits tax.

In fact, mining cannot be criticised in any respect, or the industry will saturate the airwaves with a helpful public information campaign against its misinformed critics. In short, mining—how good is it!

Minogue, Dannii As the Roman numerals at the end of Danielle Minogue's nickname indicate, she is the second member of the family to pursue global popstar fame. Like most sequels, she isn't a patch on the original.

MONA Hobart's Museum of Old and New Art, located on the Derwent River upstream from the city proper, is such an unusually excellent, eccentric and iconoclastic project that most visitors struggle to believe that such a thing could be found in Australia, let alone Tasmania. Given the origins of its iconoclastic founder David Walsh's fortune, MONA can reasonably be described as the only good thing ever to come from gambling.

Morrison, Scott A sacked Tourism Australia executive, politician and ultimately prime minister, Morrison has proved more successful at running Australia than advertising it.

As immigration minister, 'ScoMo' was a great success at turning away boats full of desperate asylum seekers fleeing persecution, and displays a statue of a typical asylum seeker fishing boat emblazoned with 'I stopped these' in his office, because he's as compassionate and gifted with empathy as many Christian ministers.

Subsequently, Morrison became **Malcolm Turnbull**'s treasurer, being handed the role that is traditionally the purview of a deputy leader even though **Julie Bishop** was

Turnbull's #2. This seems not to have been due to any overwhelming gift with numbers on Morrison's part, but rather because Morrison was seen as the most popular alternative leader, Turnbull figured that making him treasurer would tie his fate to his own.

This plan was extremely effective, with the once-popular Morrison largely disappearing except on budget night, although this had the unintended result of giving **Peter Dutton**, who had taken on Morrison's immigration profile, the space and portfolio to become Turnbull's primary internal threat instead.

Morrison unexpectedly became prime minister after Malcolm Turnbull's demise in the Liberal party room vote in 2018, because it was quickly followed by Dutton's. As improbable as this seemed, it paled in comparison to the unlikeliness of Morrison winning the 2019 federal election, leading many to wonder about the effectiveness of the power of prayer, and also what on earth God sees in Scott Morrison.

This extraordinary victory will have a lasting impact on Australian elections, which future leaders will henceforth conduct without bothering with polls, policies or colleagues.

In his early days as prime minister, Morrison has delivered on his election promise of huge tax cuts and has also been waffling about national security and religious freedom. When asked to outline in detail specific plans he would like to implement to improve the nation, however, Morrison mysteriously becomes one of the 'quiet Australians' he so reveres.

After such an improbable solo victory, Morrison seems likely to become the first PM whom his colleagues permit to finish a term since John Howard in 2007—but nowadays one can never bet against the self-destructive panicking of Australian politicians.

Motza   A substantial sum of money, generally referred to in the context of a gambling win. As such, motzas are largely fictional.

Mozzie   In a nation of deadly creatures, the mosquito may not be the most terrifying human predator but it's certainly the most prevalent, feasting on human blood and leaving itchy sores in return, which is the insect equivalent of a one-star Yelp restaurant review. Consequently, Australia's mozzies rival the Australian Christian Lobby as the nation's most perpetually irritating creatures.

Like many things, mosquitos are worse in North Queensland, where they can transmit dengue fever. Among other symptoms, this illness causes extreme tiredness, nausea and vomiting, making it quite difficult to distinguish those affected from the normal inebriated state of many North Queenslanders.

Mullet   1. A fish that is supposedly extremely surprised when stunned.

2. An Australian term used since the 1980s to describe hair that's cut short at the front and left long at the back, which has since gone global. Though never fashionable outside the realm of 1970s hair metal, and long associated with **bogans**, the American country singer Billy Ray Cyrus brought the mullet to its all-time nadir with his song 'Achy

Breaky Heart', which was number one on the ARIA chart for seven weeks in 1992.

At the time of writing, 'Old Town Road', a song featuring Billy Ray Cyrus alongside Lil Nas X, has been number one on the ARIA Charts for more than 10 weeks, and nothing makes sense anymore.

Murdoch, Rupert   A media mogul who has exercised a profound influence on Australian elections for many years, even though as a US citizen he can't vote in them. Murdoch owns popular, influential publications all over the world, and also *The Australian*. His domineering career is all the more remarkable when one remembers he only inherited one newspaper, and furthermore, that it was in **Adelaide**.

Though many of his media properties such as Fox News and *News Of The World* have attracted controversy, it's unanimously agreed that his most successful publication is the *NT News*, which delivers entertaining croc stories as reliably as *The Sun* once delivered page three nudity.

Murdoch's current (fourth) wife is the model Jerry Hall, who considers him a bastion of fidelity compared to Mick Jagger. And yet, as he's only a spring chicken of 88, Rupert Murdoch has many years ahead of him in which to accumulate three or four more ex-wives.

Muriel's Wedding   A hugely successful 1994 movie about a dullard from regional Australia who is redeemed by listening to Abba and moving to Sydney, following the trajectory of just about everyone working in the arts in Australia. Writer–director PJ Hogan bravely supplied a catchphrase that critics could use to pan the film—'You're terrible, Muriel!'—but it's a testament to his success that few of them did.

In recent years, *Muriel's Wedding* has become a successful stage musical, as its themes of small towns being toxic and Abba being awesome are just as relevant today as they were in the 1990s.

My Health Record   An innovative government platform for bringing citizens' health records online, enabling practitioners to easily access their patients' history instead of the current system of incompatible patient databases, which places a great deal of reliance on patients' defective, non-expert recollections. My Health Record is designed to lead to safer and more efficient health care for everyone, ultimately improving patient outcomes.

In practice, however, My Health Record requires citizens to entrust their precious medical records to a federal government that couldn't properly run a census after years of preparation in an era of rampant hacking and the widespread abuse of privacy by public officials, so opting out has been understandably widespread.

My Kitchen Rules   A reality TV franchise where contestants undertake the futile task of impressing a celebrity chef who believes in 'activated almonds', but not vaccines. Its name is usually abbreviated to 'MKR', because 'my kitchen rules' sounds like something a teenager from 1983 would say, and because according to one of his recent scandals, one of the rules of Pete Evans' kitchen inadvisedly involved paleo diets for babies.

Myxomatosis   A disease deliberately introduced into Australia to control the rabbit population, which it successfully reduced from 600 million to 100 million within two years of its release in 1950.

Though probably necessary, it was quite cruel to give rabbits a disease that gives them skin tumours, blindness and fever before killing them within fourteen days, when instead that fate should have been visited on Thomas Austin, the man who released 24 rabbits onto his estate in 1859 for hunting purposes, and began the current epidemic.

The current crop of rabbits are largely resistant to myxomatosis, so calicivirus has also been used, and in 2017 a Korean strain of rabbit haemorrhagic disease virus was released, because as in food and pop music, Korean rabbit ailments are so hot right now.

Nauru   Tourists are yet to flock to the island's picturesque stripped-out phosphate mine tours *(Lorrie Graham/AusAID)*

New Year's Eve   A better view of Sydney's New Year's Eve fireworks than any actual Sydneysider has ever experienced *(Adam.J.W.C.)*

Nasho National military service, or a conscript forced to undergo it, most conspicuously at the time of the Vietnam War. As a general rule, those most in favour of national service were those with no chance of being called up in the worst game of Lotto in our country's history. Back then, those forced to fight in Vietnam were looked down on because they hadn't volunteered, instead of being pitied, as is appropriate nowadays.

National Gallery of Victoria The major public art gallery in Victoria, which was once a colony, is now a state, but was never a nation, despite the gallery's grandiose title. If that weren't peculiar enough, the original St Kilda Road building is now known as 'NGV International', or in other words, 'the national gallery of a state, international'.

Nauru A territory that is legally an independent country, but whose 11,000 inhabitants are so dependent on Australia that many political scientists consider it to be a 'client state', as a substantial proportion of the country's budget comes from Australian direct aid and payments for hosting Australian immigration detention facilities. Ironically, climate change has made it likely that the inhabitants of this low-lying island may well be required to seek asylum themselves someday, and would be hoping for much kinder treatment.

One of Nauru's other major income sources is recognising breakaway territories such as Taiwan, along with Abkhazia and South Ossetia, the controversial ethnically Russian territories that have broken away from Georgia. These diplomatic initiatives have earned Nauru many millions of aid dollars, even though their recognition has not exactly proven influential.

Back when much of the island consisted of guano from bird droppings, Nauru was literally a shithole, but it's now even more unpleasant—80 per cent of the island's territory has been strip-mined for phosphate, and is an uninhabitable wasteland.

In the salad days of phosphate mining and wanton environmental degradation, Nauruans once enjoyed among the world's highest GDPs, but frittered much of their income away on bad investments. At one point their government blew several million dollars on a West End musical that portrayed a love affair between Leonardo da Vinci and Mona Lisa. It was not a critical or financial success, or a good idea.

Nauru was once known as Pleasant Island, but the name was changed, because it isn't.

NBN Originally conceived as the visionary 21st century telecommunications network of the future, delivering lightning-fast fibre-optic connections to nearly every

Australian home, the revised, updated vision for the National Broadband Network is for it to be a bit shit. It's currently falling short of this objective, as by any fair assessment it is very shit, but the NBN's management is confident that with a few more years and many more billions of dollars, it will deliver connections to 95 per cent of Australians at speeds that would have been considered fast in 1997.

New Year's Eve 31 December, which is celebrated as a party across the country.

It is traditional for all Australians to spend the last day of the year in Sydney, getting sunburnt after bagsing a choice harbourside spot, not drinking a drop of alcohol because in Sydney the cops ruin everything that even slightly resembles a party, then being unable to see 97 per cent of the fireworks because some tall dickhead who turned up at the last minute is blocking their view.

For those not in Sydney, the evening will be spent being baffled by the eccentricities of the ABC's coverage as they while away the hours leading up to the depressing realisation that they are seeing in the new year while watching fireworks on a TV screen.

Newcastle The second largest town in NSW, and the administrative but not geographical centre of the bustling Hunter region. While a significant amount of the city's CBD has been empty in recent years, some of the urban void has been filled by hipsters, whose efforts at cultural regeneration led *Lonely Planet* to name Newcastle a must-visit destination in 2011.

If this trendiness trend continues, Novocastrians could eventually become as insufferable as Melburnians—they certainly have a similar level of dislike for Sydneysiders.

Newman, Sam An ex-AFL footballer whose success in that field somehow qualified him for a long career of saying terrible things on Channel Nine. His decades of success-fully surviving controversies resulting from his horrible comments have mystified other notable players who retired with lower-profile, less lucrative respectability.

Newman's old stomping ground, the AFL *Footy Show*, was recently put out to pasture after getting roundly beaten by *The Front Bar*, a show on Channel Seven that features comedians talking about footy without needing to appal anybody. But Newman is only ever one ill-advised comeback away from getting into trouble all over again.

Nimbin A town that's always Australia's best answer to the question 'Hey man, where can I score some weed?'

No worries No problem, all is well; a common Australian reassurance or affirmation, often with 'mate' affixed. Australians are generally eager to avoid worries wherever possible, although given the present shift to casualisation and spiralling personal debt levels, this seems increasingly impossible.

NRL A sport whose players participate in excessive drinking, public nudity and the creation of amateur pornos which they exchange with one another via WhatsApp. Occasionally they put down their phones and penises, and assemble at various fields to run aggressively into one another in the name of entertaining a crowd that loves attending games as a pretext for binge drinking.

Rugby league was founded because of the then-radical idea that footballers might like to be paid for playing the game, and these radical innovators eventually became professionals, many years before the more globally popular rugby union adopted the same approach. Some rugby league clubs have taken the principle of paying players a little too far, admittedly, making huge illegal payments outside the salary cap.

Number 96 A television programme that was legendary with baby boomers for being a bit sexy, back in the days when that involved a lot of innuendo and winking instead of hardcore internet porn streamed over broadband connections. The show was set in the Sydney suburb of Paddington back when it was bohemian rather than yuppie, which certainly dates the show. It's not recorded how they came up with the number for the show's title, but the producers must have been disappointed when they realised how much sexier the show would have sounded if they'd reversed the numbers.

The show's star and top sex symbol was known only as Abigail, probably in a bid to discourage creeps from looking up her home number in the White Pages. Her character was considered hugely attractive despite being called Bev Houghton.

Oz Both Australia and Oz are fictional lands ruled by loudmouthed spin doctors *(MGM)*

Optus The one place you can reliably watch Optus Sport *(Tama Leaver)*

Obeid, Eddie A former member of NSW's Legislative Council, and also a former member of Labor—the party kicked him out for bringing it into disrepute, which he certainly did even taking into account the dubious condition of NSW Labor's reputation before the Obeid scandals.

When he was born in 1943, Obeid's parents gave him the middle name 'Moses', because he would one day lead the Labor Party into a wilderness from which it is still yet to emerge. Obeid spent twenty years in parliament, yet only rose to become Minister for Fisheries and Mineral Resources—the latter was perhaps his greatest passion, given that ICAC subsequently found he had acted corruptly in regard to a mining tenement he owned.

As well as mining, Obeid also had a great interest in water—specifically the water views from the cafés at Circular Quay whose leases he was found guilty of lobbying his former colleagues to hand over to a company secretly owned by his family. The Circular Quay tenancies were a ripe target for corruption, due to the enormous profit made available by the prime location, which provided the operators with a steady stream of price-insensitive tourists who had no idea how good Sydney cafés are meant to be.

Along with his exemplary work benefiting his family's pecuniary interests, Obeid was also prominent as a power-broker within the party, as the head of a faction known as the 'Terrigals', which originally met at his beach house in that posh coastal town—just the kind of proletarian grind that Labor's traditional working-class supporter base expects from its representatives.

As a result of his various scandals, Obeid has lost his Order of Australia Medal, his use of the honorific 'the honourable', and his liberty. Thanks to widespread disgust at his corruption, along with the multiple other scandals it experienced at the same time, Labor has lost the past three NSW elections, and counting.

Ocker   Unsophisticatedly and vulgarly Australian—in other words, Australian.

One Nation   1. A detailed modernisation agenda outlined by **Paul Keating** towards the end of his prime minister-ship, best known for the visionary objective of Australia's future lying in Asia.

2. A retrograde political party originally dedicated to lying about Asians and trying to prevent them from coming to Australia, before it abandoned that struggle to focus on preventing Muslims from coming to Australia. One Nation is also known for additional lies, such as its claim that the Great Barrier Reef is in great health, its one-time obsession with introducing a flat tax that would supposedly solve Australia's economic woes, and its claim

to an undercover Al Jazeera reporter that it could get Australia's tight gun laws relaxed in return for a hefty donation.

In recent years, One Nation's primary focus has shifted again, and it now spends much of its time on losing senators, due to both defections and breaches of the Constitution.

The party's full name is 'Pauline Hanson's One Nation', both because its founder is the party's most prominent member, and because everyone else leaves it.

Optus Australia's second national telecommunications provider from the end of Telstra's monopoly, Optus arrived in the market because the Australian government believed the industry would run more efficiently with private sector involvement. Consequently, instead of having one telco run by the Australian government, it allowed in a second telco that was majority controlled by the Singaporean government. This resulted in both lower costs for consumers, and profits being shipped overseas instead of staying in Australia, because the Singaporean government is far better at managing its commercial assets than Australia's.

— **Optus Sport** A streaming provider that has snapped up the rights to most international soccer events, Optus Sport allows its subscribers the convenience of watching live football on the device of their choice, unless more than five subscribers across the nation are doing so at once, in which case consumers will instead be given the opportunity to enjoy waiting for the stream to reconnect. Recently, Optus Sport enabled its paying subscribers not to watch such diverse events as the Champions League final, the FA Cup final and the FIFA World Cup.

After the widely publicised failure of its World Cup streaming efforts led to it being dubbed 'Floptus', Optus Sport eventually happened upon an innovative solution that enabled Australian soccer fans to catch their beloved showpiece event—giving up their expensive exclusivity to allow SBS to broadcast it as usual.

Outsiders A show on Sky News Australia that was initially presented by former federal Liberal MP Ross Cameron and federal Labor MP **Mark Latham** along with Rowan Dean, a prominent journalist with the *AFR* and *Spectator* who was already a longtime Sky News contributor. Yet somehow they managed to convince themselves that they were outsiders, despite also bragging about getting the show on the air with a single email to the head of Sky News.

Before long, however, Latham was sacked for making exactly the kind of controversial statements he was known for making in other media and, judging by the show's name, marketing and the barbed-wire background of its set, had been hired to make.

Shortly afterwards, Cameron was sacked for making racist comments, and then there was just one outsider left. Dean's colleagues had delivered on the programme's premise of making comments that aren't considered reasonable or appropriate in public. Instead of incarceration behind barbed wire, however, they presumably just had their Sky News swipe cards cancelled.

Oz Shorthand for Australia. Though spelling has varied, with 'Oss' and 'Aus' both common at one time, it's thought that the success of the *Wizard of Oz* movie helped to establish the current spelling. Furthermore, both Ozes enjoy excellent Technicolour lifestyles but are run by leaders who up close, aren't terribly impressive.

P

Parramatta   The Parramatta Eels might have had more success if they'd chosen a mascot with arms and legs *(Philippe Bourjon)*

NO THROUGH ROAD
JOINT DEFENCE FACILITY PINE GAP
PROHIBITED AREA
TURN AROUND NOW

Pine Gap   Just viewing this image of the road to the facility means you are under arrest *(Schutz)*

Packer, James Son of the legendary tycoon Kerry Packer, James fostered early doubts that he hadn't inherited his father's nous by making a disastrous investment in the doomed telco One.Tel. On assuming control of his father's empire after Kerry's death, he retrospectively burnished his father's reputation as an old-school media proprietor with a belief in quality, by deciding media was too difficult and entirely exiting the business to instead invest in casinos. Packer also had a surprisingly successful stint as a Hollywood film mogul, investing in *Gravity* among other hits, and had an unsurprisingly unsuccessful relationship with Mariah Carey.

Pademelon A smaller, stockier relative of kangaroos and wallabies that also moves by hopping. The red-bellied variety is common in Tasmania, which is generally known for having tinier versions of whatever's on the mainland. Pademelons were previously named 'philanders', literally 'human likers' in Ancient Greek, as they were considered friends to humans—a somewhat different meaning of the word to the one prevalent today. Philandering with pademelons is not recommended, and indeed, will lead to criminal charges.

Palaszczuk, Annastacia Queensland premier who made history as Australia's first woman to become premier by winning an election from opposition—the previous female premiers had all initially been appointed to the role by their colleagues in a desperate bid to stave off imminent electoral defeat for their governments.

Palaszczuk's election victory was a shock, disproving the widespread stereotype that Queenslanders would not vote for a woman, or someone called 'Annastacia Palaszczuk', or even more unlikely, Labor. As if that hadn't done enough to shatter the rest of the country's perceptions of Queensland, she won re-election in 2017.

Palmer, Clive A billionaire turned political aspirant, turned bored MP who rarely showed up to parliament, turned just plain billionaire, turned returned political aspirant who lost at the 2019 election. Palmer has a reputation for paying millions for an absurdly large quantity of political ads, and for not paying employee entitlements.

Though his political career has been erratic to say the least, his public commitment to Tim Tam and Mint Slice biscuits—the subject of many of his tweeted poems and memes, and even a mobile game he once released—has never wavered. Incidentally, some of his former employees couldn't afford to buy Tim Tams or Mint Slices.

One of Palmer's more bizarre ventures—even measured against his plans to construct a *Titanic II* and sail it on the actual ocean, where there are still actual icebergs—was his purchase of the luxurious Hyatt resort at Coolum, which he transformed into an abandoned, overgrown tropical jungle full of animatronic dinosaurs that would have resembled Jurassic Park if all of its dinosaurs had been frozen to the spot, rendering them not at all terrifying.

This plan did not prove popular with organisers of golf tournaments, who feared that if they kept hosting them at Coolum, players would find themselves hitting the ball into weird statues of dinosaurs instead of onto the fairway. Nor was it popular with the investors who were still legally obliged to make repayments on holiday villas that were subsequently closed due to the general disrepair of the resort. Some suggested that if he was so determined to 'Make Australia Great Again', in the derivative words of his 2019 campaign, he might start with his parcel of land in Coolum.

Parramatta   The oldest European settlement anywhere in the interior of Australia, Parramatta dates back to 1788, the same year that the First Fleet arrived. It has been Sydney's younger sibling, with the usual tensions, ever since.

More significantly, Indigenous Australians from the Darug nation have been in the area for at least 60,000 years and gave the city its name, which according to one possible derivation comes from the eels common to the area, where the salt water from the harbour meets the fresh waters flowing from inland.

The high frequency of these aquatic creatures gave the Parramatta Eels their mascot, although since the team has now won fourteen wooden spoons to just four premier-ships—with their most recent last place finish coming in

2018—it would be understandable if any actual Parramatta eels wanted the football club to change its name and stop embarrassing them.

Passiona   One of Australia's few home-grown soft drinks, Passiona's bright yellow colour is far more reminiscent of urine than passionfruit juice, but its unnatural sheen and carbonated bubbles make it perfect for use as a prop in any D-grade movie featuring a mad scientist's laboratory. Indeed, it was in similar circumstances that Passiona was first developed—it is only notionally passionfruit flavoured, as though it was invented by someone who had tasted passionfruit once, many years earlier, and decided to try to recreate it using only the very cheapest varieties of artificial flavouring.

Passiona is the fluid equivalent of Toobs, only with an even more scant resemblance to any natural foodstuff. It is a popular choice with anyone who wants to increase their chances of contracting diabetes and does not have access to generic supermarket-brand soft drinks.

At one point Passiona disappeared from the market, but was brought back via a retro advertising campaign informing consumers that 'It's Back!' This caused excitement with consumers who had forgotten what Passiona tasted like, but only until they tried it again.

Pell, George   A convicted paedophile.

Perth   The most remote city of its size in the world, located more than 2000 kilometres from Adelaide and even further from the nearest major city.

The Western Australian state capital was named after Perth in Scotland—which is nicknamed 'the Fair City', so it's not entirely clear to visitors in modern times why this city that is packed with dull 1980s skyscrapers got its name.

That said, Perth is justifiably known for beautiful beaches such as Cottesloe, the enjoyment of which for swimmers is only slightly undermined by the lack of enjoyment of being eaten by sharks.

Due to the enormous distance and therefore expense involved in leaving Perth, however, many of the 2 million Australians who live there are yet to do so. Perth is a heaving megalopolis compared to the rest of Western Australia, which spreads a mere 20 per cent of the state's population across 2,500,000 square kilometres.

Pine Gap A mysterious US, and notionally joint Australian, radio surveillance base located in a remote part of Central Australia. Presumably its eerie golf ball-like domes spy on anyone who thinks it might not be a great idea to have a huge, top-secret US base on Australian soil. Some conspiracy theorists believe it might house aliens, which has been denied—but then that's what they'd do if it was chock full of aliens, wouldn't they?

Piss 1. Urine.
   2. Alcohol.

— **Pissed** 1. Past participle of 'piss'.
   2. Someone who has consumed too much piss and is likely to piss any minute.

— **Piss up**   Function devoted to drinking.

— **Pissing down**   Raining heavily, in even greater volume than a urinal might experience at a piss up.

— **Piss up against a wall**   To waste money, especially if it was spent on washing the wall right before it was pissed on.

— **Piss off**   To irritate, for instance by pissing on a wall.

— **Piss it in**   To achieve something as easily as pissing in one's pants.

— **Piss poor**   This entry.

Plate   Being asked to 'bring a plate' is an instruction that requests not just the supply of a piece of crockery, but also edible items upon it. This phrase has led to confusion among recent arrivals to Australia, who may turn up to social functions brandishing either an empty plate, or if the misunderstanding is severe, a dental plate.

Plonk   Cheap, dodgy wine. It's thought that the word was corrupted from the French 'vin blanc', or white wine, by Australian troops in World War I—if so, it seems a fairly harsh review of the product obtainable from the world's top wine producer.

Australia can claim to be the nation that invented the perfect receptable for plonk—the **goon** bag.

Pom   The Australian term for a Briton, which wavers between affection and insult, just as the nation's relationship with Britain itself does. The word's evolution is quite complex: recent arrivals from the UK were once known as 'jimmygrants'—a play on the word 'immigrant'—and this transitioned to 'pomegranate', then simply 'pom'. This may not seem the height of wit, but it's less confusing than rhyming slang, at least.

Though the stigmatisation of immigrants is a problem that continues to the present day, in the case of arrivals from the UK there is an appropriate irony, given that the nation originally forced its prisoners to emigrate to Australia, and yet their descendants tend to look down on anyone who makes the same journey without wearing manacles.

Possum   Long-tailed nocturnal marsupials often found in trees, or on your roof right when you're trying to sleep, at which time they like to screech at deafening volumes. They are considered a pest in New Zealand, where they were introduced to try and establish a fur industry, and to take revenge for all the backpackers who have headed in the other direction.

— Don't stir the possum   Don't invite trouble, or create controversy. Stirring possums tends to be unwise whether or not a spoon is used to do so.

Postal survey   The most expensive and hurtful method of enacting a change, especially when polls show the thing being surveyed is overwhelmingly popular, and all sensible commentators regard the change as inevitable.

No postal survey about the wisdom of conducting postal surveys would endorse postal surveys.

Prawn   Anyone who doesn't know this word probably thinks of them as shrimp, and is wrong.

— Don't come the raw prawn with me Don't treat me like an idiot, or try to put one over me. However, the expression is sufficiently rare nowadays that using it might well make the person you are speaking to wonder whether you are in fact an idiot.

Price, Steve Another in the long line of conservative Australian broadcasters whose lack of formal education, inability to empathise with the experiences and challenges of others, and constitutional incapacity for self-doubt have made him a highly successful talkback presenter.

Unlike other shock jocks, who operate only inside a carefully curated bubble where they have the ability to talk over or even terminate any conversation where they are challenged, Price is a regular on *The Project*, where he plays the twin roles of rightist bogeyman and stuck-in-the-mud old guy for the millennials to sneer at.

The show's producers invited him on because they cleverly realised that their show would be more interesting if the presenters were confronted with the physical embodiment of everything that they're opposed to right there on the panel, instead of just in Waleed's clip packages.

Price's employer 2GB recently moved his slot from the evening to the afternoon, with the result that the former presenter in that timeslot, Chris Smith, has been required to find another employer's Christmas party at which to drunkenly harrass women.

Priscilla, Queen of the Desert, The Adventures of
A 1994 comedy film that both celebrated the legendary culture of drag shows in the Sydney gay district of Darlinghurst, and informed most of its wide-eyed viewers

about the legendary culture of drag shows in the Sydney gay district of Darlinghurst.

The story of two drag queens and a trans woman travelling to the Australian outback on a journey of personal redemption—confusingly, Priscilla was the name of a bus, rather than any of the three performers—struck a chord around the world. It was both a financial and critical success that constituted a giant step forward for historically oppressed minority groups, as long as you ignore that problematic scene with the Filipino woman and the ping pong balls.

Like the other smash hit Australian comedy from 1994, *Muriel's Wedding*, it has been turned into a successful stage musical in recent years because of its strong soundtrack, the fond memories of its audience and the near-total lack of much-loved Australian musical comedy films that followed it.

Priscilla won an Academy Award for Best Costume Design, because of course it did.

Project, The   A heaps woke current affairs show dedicated to presenting news, like, fully differently from the conventional boring newsreader approach, so it totes connects with young peeps today and has, like, a really powerful impact, you guys.

Despite this excruciating-sounding brief, the show succeeds brilliantly in delivering it.

Queenslander A typical Queenslander home. The elevation helps inhabitants stay cool and look down on southerners *(JBrew)*

AUSTRALIAN NATIVE CAT
Dasyurops maculatus

Quoll The idea that quolls are cats has proven harder to kill than this particular specimen *(Cliff)*

Queenslander 1. Somebody from Queensland, usually identifiable by their need to drop frequent mentions of Wally Lewis into conversations on any topic.

2. A house built on stilts so that the air can circulate underneath and cool the interior, allowing its inhabitants to occasionally gain some respite from the permanent hell-sauna that is the Queensland climate.

3. An expression shouted loudly and drunkenly by Queenslanders during moments of great triumph, which has the unintended effect of making those who are not Queenslanders absolutely fine with that.

Quiet Australians The beloved constituency of **Scott Morrison**, Australia's surprise prime minister, to whom he often referred favourably during the 2019 election campaign. Morrison has a symbiotic relationship with this group, as their habit of blithe contentment with the status quo is perfectly matched with his enthusiasm for maintaining it.

Morrison prefers 'quiet Australians' to the noisy ones who protest against mines and in favour of same-sex marriage instead of buckling down and working hard to build a small business that they think they need to vote Liberal to protect. Even the most basic familiarity with Morrison's own biography illustrates that he himself cannot be described as a 'quiet Australian'—especially on grand final night—but politicians never seem to feel the need to personally espouse the values they advocate for others.

Quokka   A small wallaby found principally on Rottnest Island in WA. As the name of their home is Dutch for 'rat's nest', and they bear extremely little resemblance to said rodents, they are entitled to feel a certain sense of grievance towards their state's Dutch explorer visitors. They also have a bone to pick with subsequent European arrivals to WA, as they were once widespread on the mainland before the introduction of dogs and foxes.

'Quokka' is a word in the local Nyungar language, and would have made a better name for the island as well.

Quoll   A marsupial once misnamed the 'native cat', which was ironic since domestic cats are among their major predators, and have greatly reduced their habitat—as have **cane toads**, which are substantially less cute and cuddly.

Quolls are known for having communal latrine areas which can contain many dozens of droppings, in which respect they resemble humans who attend music festivals.

R

Republic   This is why Australia will never become a republic *(gg.gov.au)*

Rain   If it rains heavily enough, you don't have to take the bin out *(Timothy Swinson)*

Rage A long-running overnight music video show on the ABC. Known for decades as a major tastemaker in the Australian music scene, and long favoured as the preferred viewing for anyone coming down after a huge night, *Rage* has survived even though everyone watches music videos on the internet nowadays. This is probably because it's very cheap to produce, and many of its clips count as local content for the purposes of quotas.

Rage's legendary status in the Australian TV industry is marred only by the programme's decades-long pronunciation of 'rage' to rhyme with 'beige'.

Rain 1. A weather phenomenon that, in Australia, is only ever too abundant or too scarce.

2. A song by Dragon that they've played so frequently since recording it in 1983 that all the moisture sweated by the band during all of the performances could fill Warragamba Dam several times over.

RBT Random breath testing, which successfully reduced the death toll on Australian roads after the failure of previous campaigns appealing to motorists' common sense.

An RBT device allows police to quickly and conveniently measure breath alcohol, and offers a handy cross-check, as while the reading is being taken, it also tests whether motorists are too **pissed** to even count to ten.

Referendum The process set out in the Australian Constitution for holding a vote that fails to change the Australian Constitution.

Republic An obvious, inevitable, necessary change that nobody seems to have the faintest idea how to achi—have you seen how cute Prince George is looking these days? Check out the palace's Instagram account! The future king is adorbs!

Rinehart, Gina Australia's richest citizen, Rinehart runs her family's mining business with acumen not immediately evident from her investments in other areas. In the media, she not only invested unsuccessfully in **Ten**, but foisted the *Bolt Report* on it; in politics, she is a long-term supporter of **Barnaby Joyce**, for reasons unclear to everybody; and in family life, she was sued by several of her own children.

In recent years she has tended to stick to what she knows best—digging holes in the ground.

Riverfire Brisbane's annual fireworks festival was originally created by Sir Joh Bjelke-Petersen as part of his effort to torch the entire city on behalf of developers. During its climax, a fighter jet flies low along the river in the centre of the city, igniting its jetstream for an extraordinary flame effect that is inexplicably yet to transform the city into the towering inferno Joh so badly wanted in order to offer his cronies a 'remarkable green-fields opportunity'. Admittedly, such a fire would have the benefit of removing all the hideous buildings and freeways he approved.

Roberts, Malcolm The One Nation senator for Queensland who isn't Pauline Hanson, Roberts was re-elected in 2019 despite previously being thrown out of parliament for not having renounced his overseas citizen-ship, and despite him being decidedly odd even compared to other One Nation figures.

Roberts wrote letters to the prime minister which bore eccentric: punctuation-marks commonly associated with the extremist, ultra-libertarian sovereign citizen move-ment. He has denied knowing of this movement, and to be fair to him, it's plausible that every single punctuation mark was a typo.

Perhaps Queensland voters were eager to return him to the Senate to spend more time advancing eccentric climate denial theories and holding bizarre hearings into the UN's plans for a sinister world government? It's certainly true that Roberts' return to the Australian parliament makes the notion of being governed by an oligarchical cabal funded by mega-wealthy bankers seem like a vastly superior option.

Rogaining 1. A sport from Melbourne that involves cross country wayfinding, which resembles orienteering.

2. A sport involving applying expensive medicine to your hair so you won't go bald.

Rort To defraud, cheat, embezzle or otherwise treat somebody in the same way that major Australian banks routinely treat their customers, as revealed in the recent banking royal commission.

S

Same-sex marriage   Its legalisation has forced *Q&A* to find new topics
(Paris Buttfield-Addison)

Shoey   Surely someone like Daniel Ricciardo who drives around in one of
these could afford a drinking glass? *(Morio)*

Same-sex marriage The debate over whether to legalise gay marriage dominated Australian politics for many years, during which period nearly all similar overseas jurisdictions managed to do so, and yet conservatives on both sides of politics continued to insist that a silent majority opposed it—an extremely silent one, given the many opinion polls that made it absolutely clear that most Australians supported changing the laws.

Bids to do so during the Rudd–Gillard period fell short of votes, given the opposition maintained by many in the Catholic right of the Labor party.

In 2017, rather than simply doing the right, obvious and inevitable thing and just changing the law, the Turnbull government instead decided to invite every Australian to vote on the proposal in a non-binding '**postal survey**'.

This proposal had been dreamed up by the well-known same-sex marriage opponent and mathematical genius **Peter Dutton**, who hoped that millennials and other young people would fail to vote because of their inability to understand what a letter or post office is. His gambit certainly delayed the decision for nearly a year.

Like most of Dutton's recent plans involving numbers and votes, however, his calculation ultimately failed catastrophically, and the 'yes' case won comfortably, gaining 61 per cent of the vote. However, Dutton's plan did succeed in inflicting months of hateful rhetoric on the gay community, as the advocates of the 'no' case went about exhaustively proving the tenet that there are no good arguments against same-sex marriage.

Same-sex marriage was legalised in 2017, shortly after the result was announced, and since then the world has ended, the sky has fallen in, people have started marrying animals and the Sydney Harbour Bridge, and every child in Australia has been irrevocably corrupted, just as same-sex marriage's opponents warned.

Sandilands, Kyle   A contrarian radio broadcaster who first came to prominence when Jackie O's radio station wanted to replace Jackie's ex-husband 'Ugly Phil' O'Neil with someone who had an ugly personality as well as appearance. Kyle has created controversy ever since, but in Sydney, broadcasters who regularly make disturbing comments are only ever embraced all the more warmly by radio audiences.

Kyle is now such an institution that he has few targets left to be iconoclastic towards, and has even developed something of a soft side in recent years, offering jobs to radio executives from other networks who got sacked because they went streaking at the footy. If he gets much mellower, he may end up making his next move to Smooth FM.

Sandpaper The preferred product for Australians seeking to smooth out bumpy surfaces to prepare them for painting, add roughness to a surface to improve the bonding of glue, or plunge the nation into a profound crisis of self-examination after several of our most successful cricketers are exposed as cheats.

Sauce Liquor, as in the phrase 'on the sauce'. Australian drinking also features sauce at the end of the night, when it traditionally appears in its tomato or barbecue forms on a late-night kebab. Even more decadent a sauce experience can be found in the halal snack pack, which features no less than three squeeze-pack sauces—chili, barbecue and garlic.

— **Fair suck of the sauce bottle** An Australian idiom that's roughly equivalent to demanding a 'Fair go!' but is both more evocative and confusing, suggesting as it does a scenario where people pass around a bottle of sauce and are supposed to suck out an equal amount. That image makes more sense if the 'sauce' in question is the alcoholic variety.

Kevin Rudd was mocked for saying 'fair shake of the sauce bottle' instead, in keeping with his strong preference for speaking in old-fashioned, slightly mangled idioms. But while definitely more obscure, Rudd's version in fact makes more sense, given the known impossibility of dislodging tomato sauce from bottles without vigorous shaking, tapping or even sticking a sharp object in the little hole.

Sausage roll A breakthrough in culinary technology whereby sausages and their surrounding sandwiches were fused into one product—a tube of sausage meat encased in crumbly pastry that immediately covers every nearby surface as soon as you open the packet. The sausage roll is ubiquitous in Australia's **servos** and **corner stores**, and the experience of eating one is always the same—your mouth turns instantly dry, and you wish you'd bought a meat pie instead.

'Party' sausage rolls and meat pies are also commonly served at Australian social functions, because they take almost no effort to defrost, taste mostly of tomato sauce and handily soak up the six beers everyone is drinking.

SBS The Special Broadcasting Service is Australia's multicultural public broadcaster, albeit often only conceptually nowadays. SBS is expected by the government to achieve the contradictory aims of maintaining its niche foreign language programming and achieving a significant proportion of its funding from advertising.

Popular recent programmes include a reality show featuring the deportation of racists, *Go Back To Where You Came From*, which went on to inspire Donald Trump's notorious tweets to Democratic congresswomen. SBS also won large audiences during the last FIFA World Cup, and the World Cup before that, and indeed the World Cup before that.

SBS runs many of the stations in other languages that people skip past when surfing around the radio dial, and 'SBS Viceland', a youth-oriented TV channel that is somehow both publicly owned by Australian taxpayers and bears the brand of a private American channel co-owned by Disney.

Scallops   1. Edible mollusc.

2. Deep-fried battered potato cakes. Having the same word for two such different fish and chip shop food items doesn't make sense, but in the interests of irrationally asserting that his home region's usage is the best, the author will fight anyone who reckons they're called something more sensible like a 'potato cake' or 'potato fritter'.

Schoolies Week   A traditional Australian rite of passage where young people gather at beaches after their final exams to celebrate their newly adult ability to do whatever they want by contracting alcohol poisoning.

This drunken celebration of their newfound freedom is always accompanied by an even more troubling tradition where Schoolies events are infiltrated by creepy older men known as Toolies, many of whom are subsequently deprived of their own freedom by courts of law.

ScoMo   An abbreviation for **Scott Morrison** designed to make him seem like a daggy surburban dad, but which sounds uncomfortably like 'Scummo'.

Screamer   1. A very impressive overhead mark (catch) in Australian Rules football, also known as a 'speccie', short for 'spectacular mark'. A player might take 'an absolute screamer', for instance, but would generally refrain from screaming after doing so.

2. A 'two-pot screamer' is someone who gets drunk easily, as two pots equates to two fairly small beers. Somebody who took a screamer and won a game of footy for their teammates would not want to be a two-pot screamer when celebrating.

Scull/skull/skoll   A popular Australian war cry, where the battle is against an unconsumed receptacle of alcohol, and victory is obtained by somebody consuming it as fast as humanly possible while a group of fellow soldiers cheers them on.

As soon as the group's target accedes to the repeated chanting of the word and begins drinking, the group will next sing a charming ditty about how the drinker in question is 'true blue', 'a pisspot through and through', reputed to be a 'bastard', and doomed to hell, before demanding that they 'drink it down'.

Peer pressure has been identified as one of the causes of drinking problems.

Seachange   Someone who moves to the coast to chill out, emulating the characters from the TV series *SeaChange*, because all major life decisions should be based on fictional characters in middle-class ABC drama shows that get ill-advisedly rebooted on Channel Nine.

In recent years, however, seachanges have become more rare, because coastal properties have become just as horrifically overpriced as buying in the city. It is not recorded how many people made seachanges purely because they wanted to hook up with a guy who looked like David Wenham.

The term 'tree change' is also used for somebody who moves from the city to the **bush**, but the expression is best avoided due to it being a horrific pun.

Section 44(i) A Section of the Australian Constitution that prevents dual citizens from serving in the parliament. The recent shenanigans that saw fifteen politicians punted from the parliament because of it has made 44(i) the clear winner of the prize for the most entertaining subsection in the entire Constitution, admittedly against extremely minimal competition.

Seekers, The The first Australian musical group to achieve worldwide success, the group was formed in 1962, were named Australians of the Year in 1967, and broke up in 1968, possibly because being named Australians of the Year extinguished their last remaining shreds of commercial credibility. The group has reunited regularly, however, and in 2019 recorded the album *Farewell* which is supposedly their last, putting paid to the widespread rumours that the group is immortal.

Servo An abbreviation of 'service station' that has been retained long after petrol stations stopped offering any. Besides petrol, Aussies go down to the servo for ice, bait and snacks—all arguably fuels of a different kind.

Shag 1. A seabird often seen alone by the coast, hence the expression 'like a shag on a rock', meaning 'to be left alone'.
2. Having sex. As opposed to the first meaning, anybody who has a shag on a rock has obviously not been left alone.

Sheep's back   The place where Australia was supposed to have ridden, economically speaking. The phrase suggests that the nation merely coasts on the efforts of farmers, which has been challenged in recent years by ads from the Minerals Council that suggest Australians now ride on the miner's back. Given how challenging it would presumably be for any Australian to successfully ride on a sheep's back without it objecting stridently, however, it's possible that this metaphor needs rethinking.

Sheila   Originally referring to an Irish woman, the word now means a woman in general, which has led to Australians not wanting to call their daughters Sheila because it seems so generic.

Shelton, Lyle   The former head of the Australian Christian Lobby until he quit to waste his time running for the Senate, earning less than 1 per cent of the vote. Shelton is a staunch defender of the parts of the Bible where it says that homosexuality is bad, and less so the parts about loving thy neighbour as thyself, judging not, that ye be not judged, and not trying to remove the speck of sawdust in someone else's eye until you've gotten rid of the plank located in your own.

Given the abject failure of all his recent campaigns, including his effort to stop the legalisation of same-sex marriage, it can only be concluded that God isn't on Lyle's side, and has most likely judged him to be a bit of a dick.

What's more, as the Australian Conservatives, the party he was running for, was disbanded by its founder Cory Bernardi after its stunning lack of success at the 2019 elections, it seems likely that God is sending Lyle a stern message about doing something else with his life.

Shoey Popularised by F1 driver Daniel Ricciardo, a 'shoey' involves consuming an alcoholic beverage such as champagne from the shoe you just wore during your race.

The rise of the shoey is evidence that Australians will drink whenever they can, even when they've just finished a gruelling race and the only drinking receptacle available is a disgusting-smelling shoe.

The trend of a victor drinking champagne from their sweaty boot is nevertheless less silly than racing's previous victory tradition of wasting the champagne by spraying it everywhere.

Shorten, Bill A Labor politician whose career trajectory has taken him from being the parliamentary secretary in charge of the push for the National Disability Insurance Scheme in 2007 to a lesser position, twelve years later, as Shadow Minister for it.

Shorten was elected Labor leader in 2013 despite ordinary members not voting for him in the party's first-ever leadership ballot, and almost elected prime minister in 2016 despite ordinary voters not liking him. His shock 2019 election loss was a belated reminder that success in politics generally requires some degree of popularity.

Despite the anguish of his two election losses, Shorten will stay in politics in the hope of being a senior minister in a future Labor government led by someone popular, whom he can then successfully challenge in the party room, becoming PM at last.

Sickie   A day spent at home pretending to be sick, so as to get out of going to work, school or a social obligation. Sickies are most commonly, and suspiciously, taken on Mondays, Fridays and days falling in between public holidays and weekends. It's understood that sickies are an absolute right for Australian workers, because after all, the boss takes them as well.

The major inspiration for taking sickies is being extremely hungover, which tends to produce some of the symptoms of a legitimate illness such as nausea and fatigue, but for which, regrettably, most doctors will not issue medical certificates. The benefit of hangovers is that they make the person fabricating the illness sound genuinely unwell—the downside is that because they feel genuinely unwell, it's often difficult to enjoy their day off.

— **Chuck a sickie**   The act of organising a sickie for oneself, which used to require calling your boss and pretending to have a nasty sore throat so that they'd tell you to stay home, but has become much easier with the advent of email and SMS.

This is distinct from being genuinely sick, which can also sometimes involve chucking.

Skip   1. An Australian, originally used for those of British descent, but now used more generally. This term was developed by 'skips' themselves from 'skippy'—a term for a kangaroo long before the TV show—as a less hateful alternative to the contemptuous names that Australian-born people were called by those who were British-born, such as **currency lad/lass**.

2. A giant bin, such as those used on building sites, into which British-born snobs are most welcome to jump.

Sky News   A fun-sized, yet not fun, news channel that, despite its teeny-tiny audience, broadcasts high-quality reportage and must-see political coverage, but only during daylight. During the evening prime time hours, Sky News replaces its renowned news coverage with hours of angry shouting, which rates so much more strongly than its news content that it's only a matter of time before the channel gives up on expensive journalists and live crosses, and simply broadcasts rage 24/7.

Sky's commentary line-up features many respected former Liberal MPs and staffers, a smattering of Labor figures, generally to serve as punching bags, and Bronwyn Bishop to offer comic relief by bleating implausibly about creeping socialism.

— **Sky Business Channel**   A second Sky News offering whose only apparent purpose was to make the main channel look high-rating by comparison. It ultimately closed because it wasn't a very good business.

Sledge   A term originating from cricket, where it referred to breaking a batter's concentration through sustained insults. Sledging used to be considered jolly fair play by the Australian men's cricket team, but in the aftermath of the recent cheating scandal, the team has tried to stamp out its use. This may be because of a genuine attempt to lift their standards of sportsmanship, or it may simply be the case that the team is no longer capable of using sledging to put off its opponents, because every insult offered can be shrugged off by simply mentioning the word **sandpaper**.

There is a theory that the term evolved from the name of the singer Percy Sledge, because of a very classy example where a fielding team sang 'When A Man Loves A Woman' as a batsman whose wife was supposedly cheating on him took to the field. By modern standards, this would be considered a uselessly subtle sledge.

Smashed   1. Damaged to the point of destruction.
   2. Consumed very rapidly.
   3. Epically drunk.
   4. Spread lavishly on toast at breakfast time.

Smith, Steve Australia's best batsman since Don Bradman, as well as the entire game's, at least judging by the ICC rankings. Like the Don, he has a highly unorthodox style relying on exceptional coordination, and would have scored more runs but for a regrettable interruption to his career.

Admittedly, Bradman's legendary career was cut short by World War II, whereas Smith's was put on hold by his suspension, which resulted from his role in an idiotic ball-tampering plot, so the situations aren't entirely comparable.

When not being penalised for turning a blind eye to the abjectly stupid plan to use **sandpaper** to scuff up a ball in front of high definition cameras, however, Smith is as placid and reliable a run-accumulator as any team could wish for.

While he was booed by crowds after returning from suspension, it's possible that some of his many critics would feel more sympathy for the former captain if they knew that he had already been punished with the middle name 'Devereux'.

Smith cannot be considered for a leadership position until twelve months after his suspension finishes, at which time he will instantly replace whichever unfortunate is in the role at the time, because while Australian cricket despises ball-tampering, it's still very keen on winning.

Sorry Day 26 May each year, when Australians remember the immense harm done by forcibly removing Aboriginal children from their families, which created what became known as the 'Stolen Generation'.

The date commemorates 26 May 1997, when the landmark *Bringing Them Home* report detailing the problem was issued by the then Human Rights and Equal Opportunities Commission. (This has been renamed the Human Rights Commission, as most Australians no longer care about equal opportunities.)

Some of the apologies offered on National Sorry Day should be made by those responsible for the Australian government not apologising for a policy that was tantamount to genocide until 2008.

Spit the dummy 1. To lose your temper, like **Bernard Tomic** at a press conference.

2. To give up, like **Bernard Tomic** in a tennis tournament.

Spunkrat Someone much more attractive than the image implies.

Squatter 1. Someone who grazed livestock on publicly owned land without permission, and was ultimately given ownership of the land, becoming wealthy and powerful as a result.

2. Someone who lives in an abandoned house due to poverty, and is liable to be evicted at any time, because nowadays people aren't just allowed to grab land in Australia, even though both the farming squatters and the First Fleet did.

— **Squatters' rights** Under the law of adverse possession, somebody can take permanent control of land they've effectively controlled for at least twelve years. Under this rule, Queensland came perilously close in the early 2000s to keeping the State of Origin trophy forever.

—**Squattocracy** Some squatters, who eventually became the social elite of the colonies, were derisively described as a '**squattocracy**'. A similarly dismissive term for those who wanted to be considered the new colonies' aristocrats was 'bunyip aristocracy', which referred to a proposal for an Australian peerage made by W.C. Wentworth, rather than actual bunyip aristocrats, which would have been far more entertaining.

Stefanovic, Karl The long-time co-host of Nine's *Today Show*, Karl was popular with viewers for his jolly on-screen antics, like his tipsy performance the morning after the Logies, or confusing the Dalai Lama by telling him a joke about the Buddhist leader walking into a pizza shop and asking them to make him one with everything.

But Stefanovic's star began to wane when he became known for less jolly off-screen antics, like breaking up with the mother of his three children and being overheard complaining about his new co-host, and *Today*'s producers made him one with unemployment. He has remained as host of Nine's show *This Time Next Year*, but given its flagging ratings at the time of writing, probably won't work there at all this time next year.

Stefanovic, Peter The younger and less famous Stefanovic brother who also worked for Channel Nine presenting *Weekend Today* until he too was let go in the Great Stefanovic Purge of 2018.

During his time at the network, Peter's most famous interview was in an Uber, with his brother.

Steggall, Zali The barrister-turned-independent candidate who unseated Tony Abbott in his Sydney seat of Warringah at the 2019 election. More painfully still for the former prime minister, her Olympic slalom medal means she also comfortably outdoes him in terms of sheer athleticism.

Straya The correct pronunciation of 'Australia'. Any other pronunciation will give rise to suspicions that the speaker is not a true, **dinky-di** Australian, or more troublingly still, might be a posho from Adelaide.

Streaking Also known as a nuddy or nudie run, taking one's clothes off and running through the middle of a sporting event is a time-honoured Australian larrikin tradition, and incredibly annoying if your team is behind.

Streaking has become less common in recent years, however, as authorities introduced crippling fines and even gaol sentences in some cases, while broadcasters have been required to point their cameras away from streakers' bits so as not to encourage others. The biggest reason behind the decline in streaking, however, is that internet porn has made looking at nudity so commonplace that audiences no longer cheer streakers, but instead complain that the content isn't hardcore enough.

Strewth 1. An oath, abbreviated from 'It's truth'.
2. The only good bit of *The Australian*.

Struggle Street A roadway visible only to broadcaster Alan Jones, whose hypothetical residents' concerns he enthusiastically advocates once he has dealt with those of his sponsors and mates on the political right. While Struggle Street's exact location is unclear, it's definitely a long way from Jones' residence right beside the Sydney Opera House.

Stubby A short beer bottle, designed to resemble a traditional beer stein, and with a shorter and flatter size than traditional, longer-necked bottles to make them easier to pack and transport. Once ubiquitous among Australian drinkers, the stubby flame is now mostly kept alive by Victoria Bitter.

— **Stubby holder** A dual purpose item that keeps a beer cool while displaying a fashionable design. For traditional Australian men, their stubby holder is the only item that's ever permitted to be decorated ornately.

— **Darwin stubby** A giant glass beer bottle, originally introduced in 1958 as 80 imperial fluid ounces (2270 millilitres) because it was easier to transport larger containers across long distances.

More recently, NT Draught was available in a slightly more restrained 2-litre container. The Darwin Stubby was discontinued entirely by Carlton and United Breweries in 2015, leading to an outcry among many Territorians who still preferred to consume their beer in ludicrously oversized bottles. These absurdly hardcore drinkers presumably now drink direct from the barrel.

— **A stubby short of a six pack** Somebody stupid, or not all there. The phrase is somewhat confusing, because someone who drinks all six beers is likely to behave more foolishly than someone who's had five.

— **Stubbies** A brand of shorts known for being as practical as they are unflattering, and often worn by people who consume stubbies when they knock off from work.

Sullivan's Cove A small-batch whisky distilled in **Hobart**, Tasmania that was named the world's best single malt in 2014. It takes its name from the main stretch of harbour on Hobart's waterfront, which is a well-known place for local drinkers to congregate at waterside bars where it's warm enough to drink outdoors for as many as six weeks of the year.

Sullivan's Cove has been at the vanguard of Tasmania's development into a well-known whisky producing area, alongside other successful producers like Lark, Nant and Hellyer's Road. Tasmania has turned out to be ideal for whisky production because much of the island is remote, dark, cold, damp and miserable, just like the Scottish Highlands.

Summernats The peak annual event for Australian hoons and bogans, Summernats is a motoring festival that is the only déclassé event that ever takes place in Canberra. Over 100,000 people gather for the four-day festival, which has a reputation for burnout contests, elaborate custom paint jobs and sexual harassment.

Sunnyboy A pyramidical frozen ice confection. While they were widely consumed in the nation's tuckshops back in the era where it was perfectly reasonable for children to consume a mix of sugar and food colouring at recess, their major value was as a playground weapon, as their sharp point and frozen heft made them an unpleasant object with which to be bonked on the head. It's not clear whether it was the ingredients' lack of nutritional value or its easy adaptation into a playground cosh that led to the Sunnyboy's demise.

— **The Sunnyboys** An Australian band whose best-known hit is 'Alone With You Tonight', a poignantly sad song about the loneliness that follows from being hospitalised with a head injury caused by an orange-flavoured pyramid of ice.

Swimmers Cossies.

Sydney The largest city in Australia for at least a few more years until Melbourne overtakes it, this once fun, pleasant city has been successfully transformed into a bustling metropolis crammed with builders constructing new luxury high-rise developments by day, and a ghost town by night, in accordance with the demands of the city's powerful developercrats.

Thanks to their efforts, the quintessential Sydney night out now involves looking down from the balcony of a 40th-floor apartment in a new inner-city block that has a 24 hour concierge, private cinema, sauna and golf simulator, sipping Aperol Spritzes as you gaze at the bobbing lights of the boats on the harbour and listen to the gentle lapping of the waves against the foreshore, uninterrupted by the slightest noise from anything resembling nightlife, because the 150-year-old pub around the corner closed down after years of relentless noise complaints from everyone in your building.

While many Sydneysiders have relocated to south-east Queensland or Melbourne, many more have remained in their city. Some stay because their houses have accumulated so much value that they reason Sydney must still be a great place to live even though it doesn't feel like one, while others remain because they've bought off the plan and can't afford to escape even though they're certain their completed residence will have potentially fatal defects. More still have contracted Stockholm Syndrome and simply can't imagine escaping a place which objectively makes them miserable.

Sydney's beaches are still pleasant, as they remain a strong pull factor for apartment purchasers, but parking never is. What's more, catching a train to Bondi Beach instead of a horribly slow bus remains impossible because selfish locals opposed the line's extension.

Sydney does, however, still put on a huge **New Year's Eve** party, like a jaded lounge singer who still drags themselves out to perform occasionally because that's just about all they have left. It is, in fact, all Sydney has left.

— **Sydney Metro** A new train line in Sydney that is an example of **economic rationalism** in action. Rather than being operated by the public sector like most Australian public transport networks, the Metro was outsourced to a private company majority-owned by the MTR Corporation from Hong Kong, which is majority-owned by the Hong Kong government, which is ultimately part of the communist People's Republic of China. It seems, then, that the NSW government is happy with socialised public ownership as long as the public doing the owning is in another, socialist, country.

T

Tigerair A plane in its natural delayed environment *(YSSYguy)*

Trakkies Australia's Olympic softballers in their formal paradewear *(paddynapper)*

Tall poppy An especially successful person, who by long-standing Australian custom gets cut down to size through mockery and undermining. In this way, the nation's famous egalitarian spirit is preserved by preventing anyone from becoming unequal on account of their talent or success. While this tends to prevent excellence, it's surely a small price to pay to protect the egos of those who have been less successful.

In recent years the 'tall poppy syndrome' has repeatedly been applied to prime ministers, who get cut down by their colleagues after a year or two no matter how successful they are in the job.

Ten A television network that broadcasts its programmes 24 hours a day just in case anyone ever wants to watch one.

Terra nullius A doctrine in international law that specifies 'finders keepers' for any parcel of land that was previously uninhabited. As applied to Australia by the British colonial administration—that is, illegally in terms of international law—it meant 'land containing no other white people'.

Tigerair   A low cost carrier that is ideal for passengers who don't mind a little adversity in exchange for a cheap flight, and enjoy the excitement of wondering if they'll end up travelling on the day they booked.

Tiger is now fully owned by Virgin, and in keeping with the parent company's brand, many passengers wonder whether it's their cabin crew's first time running an aircraft.

Tinny/tinnie   1. A can of beer.

2. A metal dinghy. To add to the confusion, tinnies are frequently consumed aboard tinnies, and neither kind is made from tin.

Togs   Bathers.

Tomic, Bernard   A young tennis star whose immense natural gifts sometimes let him win tennis matches on those rare occasions when he doesn't pull out of them or display the '50 per cent effort' he once boasted about in a media interview. As a junior, Tomic notoriously claimed he would become world number one some day, and yet his all-time best ranking so far has been 17, briefly. This hasn't stopped him from bragging about the millions he's earned from the game—as opposed to the respect he hasn't.

Trakkies   Australian formalwear. Tracksuit pants, or 'trakkie daks', are traditionally worn with t-shirts, as the zips on trakkie tops can be fiddly, and if you dress in matching top and bottoms, it feels a little too much like you've put serious thought into your appearance instead of delving through a disorganised clothes drawer at the last minute.

In all parts of Australia besides fashionable Melbourne, tracksuit pants may be worn at any event, whether a wedding, funeral, job interview or your own investiture into the Order of Australia—everyone present will understand that the wearer's desire for comfort overwhelmed any requirement for formality, and will probably be wearing trakkies themselves, or wishing they were. Even prime ministers can wear trakkie daks, as John Howard proved on far too many occasions.

In terms of matching footwear, the trakkie dak wearer has a free choice between sneakers, **Ugg boots** and thongs.

Trakkies may be obtained from such well-known high fashion retailers as Kmart, Target, Big W and Lowes. It would be extravagant to pay more than $10 for a pair.

Owning trakkies is not all upside, however—they tend to fall down once they get older and the elastic goes, and you tend to lose one end of the drawstring inside the waistband.

triple j The national youth broadcaster, known for playing music that's popular with young Australians, and also Australian hip-hop.

Tropfest Initially named for the Tropicana Caffe, a local Darlinghurst eatery where actor John Polson screened a few short films for friends in 1993, Tropfest was once a must-attend summer event that drew huge crowds to screening sites across the country and even across the world. Ultimately, the crowds began to realise that nearly every film contained one joke and a celebrity cameo, and grew tired of the format.

Tropfest continues today in **Parramatta**, if it can be called continuing.

Troppo   Crazy, described as 'gone troppo'. The term is commonly thought to have been coined by Australian troops stationed in the Pacific during World War II, where they formed a belief that long exposure to tropical conditions sent people crazy. A more plausible derivation, however, is that the term was coined by visitors to North Queensland.

Trots   1. Harness races, during which the horses' legs are restricted so they can't accelerate to a gallop, presumably to remove the excitement of horses running fast so that the hardcore punters who follow the sport can focus entirely on the tedious maths of calculating odds.

2. Members of the political far-left, or Trotskyists, most of whom actively despise pastimes that real working-class people enjoy, such as harness racing.

True blue   Genuinely Australian, as distinct from the Madonna song 'True Blue'. The original derivation was British, and meant 'staunchly conservative'—later Australian usage meant 'a staunch unionist', perhaps because of the Eureka flag.

But of course that meaning is not popular nowadays, like unions themselves—so the term now means 'true to Australian values', which tends to mean either left- or right-wing ones depending on who's appealing to them.

Turnbull, Malcolm   A socially progressive, technocratic politician whose first term as Liberal leader was cut abruptly short because he didn't listen to his colleagues enough. His second term, when he challenged Tony Abbott and became PM, was cut abruptly short because he did nothing but listen to his colleagues, which inspired him to take minimal action on many of his popular positions so as to keep them on side. The conservative wing of the party still hated him anyway, and eventually succeeded in dumping him—ironically because his personal popularity had dropped as a result of his strategic inaction.

Turnbull's significant achievements as a barrister and personal wealth from his time as a merchant banker made him the best embodiment of the Liberal values of hard work, small business and personal success of any of the party's MPs in years—however, working with him led many Liberals to conclude that someone with just a little bit less personal success would be fine, thanks.

Turps   1. Being 'on the turps' means boozing, although preferably not literally on turpentine.

2. Ian 'Turps' Turpie, the legendary game show host and singer responsible for the album *Turps Is The Talk Of The Town*. Turps died in 2012 but lives on in the hearts of all who watched *The Go!! Show* and *The New Price Is Right*. Not so much *Supermarket Sweep*.

Twelve Apostles   A series of limestone rock formations off the Victorian coast that is one of the major tourist attractions along the Great Ocean Road. The name is confusing—some might say 'stupid'—because there were only eight when the name was given, and erosion has reduced the number to seven.

It might be simplest just to rename them the Approximately Half Dozen Apostles so as to reduce disappointment, although in fairness, the number does accurately reflect the number of Jesus' apostles after the first five were killed.

U

Ugg boots Available in a wide range of appalling styles *(Snowball181)*

Ute This Toyota Hilux might not quite live up to its 'high luxury' promise

Uey Pronounced 'ewe ee', this is an abbreviation for a U-turn, which is generally described as being 'chucked'.

Metaphorical policy U-turns are also frequently made by governments—although they are generally described as backflips, which seems a worse analogy because after a backflip, you're facing exactly where you started.

Ugg boots Sheepskin footwear worn only by **bogans** and tourists seeking to buy a traditional Australian product. While the fleecy interior makes them comfortable, the same can be said of slippers, which should not be worn out of the house—just like the Ugg boot.

Uluru Statement From The Heart A cautiously worded, eminently reasonable request that the centuries of Indigenous oppression in this country be counteracted by a permanent 'voice to parliament' to ensure that, as has so rarely occurred in the past, First Nations views will be heard as a matter of course in the future.

Successive governments have dismissed the idea out of hand as being a 'third chamber of parliament', which was never countenanced, and just goes to show that even if a body composed of Indigenous Australians is ever allowed to speak to the federal parliament, it remains unlikely that governments will listen to it.

Un-Australian   The most indefensible Strayan crime imaginable, along with being a **dobber**. Nobody knows precisely what being 'Australian' means, besides some vague banalities about the 'fair go' and 'mateship', with frequent references to the ANZAC spirit, overlooking the fact that many ANZACs were New Zealanders. But the term 'un-Australian' is nevertheless considered a vehement denouncement of anyone seen to have betrayed what we stand for, whatever that is.

Ute   The iconic tradie's 'utility' vehicle, utes are mandatorily used to transport gravity-defying dogs who somehow stay in the tray. In America, the ute is known as a 'pick-up truck'; Australians are traditionally more in favour of picking up in panel vans.

In 2019, the top three vehicles sold in Australia were all utes, for the first time in many years. A smaller number than ever were bought by actual tradies, as opposed to male stockbrokers with a wildly inaccurate self-image.

V

Vivid Sydney This photo of the Vivid lights would look less unimpressive if we'd printed the book in colour *(Robert Montgomery)*

Very Fast Train The XPT is, technically speaking, a not-very-fast train *(Bidgee)*

Verandah over the toy shop A big male gut. Anyone wondering can probably figure out by themself what the toy shop metaphor is supposed to represent, and subsequently vomit.

Very Fast Train A high-speed rail line that would link Melbourne to Brisbane via Canberra and Sydney is one of Australia's long-rumoured yet mythical beings, alongside bunyips, yowies and reasonably-priced inner-city housing.

Virgin Australia Part of the national aviation duopoly along with Qantas Group, the airline, whose fleet was initially painted bright red, began in 2000 as Virgin Blue in honour of the perennially lame Australian joke where someone with red hair is known as '**Bluey**'.

Shortly after its foundation, the collapse of Ansett and Impulse Airlines left Virgin as the only competitor to Qantas—this enabled the airline to expand significantly, and largely abandon its market position as a plucky challenger, offering business class and lounges, until it eventually became almost indistinguishable from Qantas, and almost as experienced.

Vivid Sydney   An annual winter festival of lights, music, ideas and crowds. Although they were the festival's original focus, the light shows now primarily serve to placate the long queues waiting to catch public transport home.

W

Westfield The vast mall in the background is probably linked to the 'for lease' signs in the foreground

Western Sydney Airport Western Sydney International Airport, pictured in 2014 (*Advanstra*)

'Waltzing Matilda' The most famous verse by A.B. 'Banjo' Paterson advocates suicide as a means of avoiding the consequences of crime, which is possibly not the ideal message for our most beloved national song.

Wanker Someone who derives pleasure from attempting to impress with their social superiority and erudition, but instead just makes people suspect that they've got their hand on it, probably literally. Synonyms include tosser, pretentious git and Pete Evans.

Watts, Naomi An actress who would be a much better person with whom to share a lamb roast than Tom Cruise. She has starred in many critically acclaimed, box office smash hit movies, and also *The Ring Two*.

Watts spent part of her childhood in Wales, and attended Ysgol Gyfun Llangefni school, which remarkably isn't a typo. She thinks of herself as British, and has spent many years living in America, but she is sufficiently connected to Australia by her teens, the early stages of her career and at least some shreds of her accent for us to claim her, just in case she finally wins that Oscar.

It must be acknowledged, though, that Watts has already brought some honour to both of her homelands with her stunning victory in the 2002 Fangoria Chainsaw Awards— almost enough for her to be forgiven for her appearance in *I ♥ Huckabees*.

Weaving, Hugo A hugely versatile Australian actor whom, despite his immense talent, nobody can unsee as the terrifying Agent Smith from *The Matrix*, and can we really be sure he still isn't working for the machines, deep undercover? No, we can't. Take the red pill, Australia.

Western Sydney The rapidly growing region to the west of Sydney's crowded coastal suburbs that contains 10 per cent of Australia's population and consumes 100 per cent of its focus during federal elections.

— Western Sydney Airport A new international airport that will enable the residents of Western Sydney to travel overseas without conducting the long commute to the city's original coastal airport. Despite decades of arguments over its location, residents decided to stop protesting when it was pointed out to them that once it was open, they wouldn't have to travel overseas with wankers from the Eastern Suburbs.

In keeping with the demands of its local market, flights from Western Sydney Airport will go only to Bali and Phuket.

The airport will be known as Nancy-Bird Walton International Airport, following rules set for Kingsford-Smith Airport that require all terminals in the region to be named after a famous aviator with a hyphenated name.

Westfield   A global shopping mall brand that began life in a paddock in Blacktown in 1959—a Western Sydney field, in other words.

The company soon began to replicate itself and spread across the globe in a manner reminiscent of the influenza virus, constantly evolving to overcome consumer resistance. One of Westfield's early victims was the Sydney suburb of Bondi Junction, which is now overrun by a giant multi-building mall that will someday absorb those few parts of its shopping district not currently contained within the air-conditioned Westfield corridors.

Nowadays, giant Westfields can be found from the US to Europe. The company took over management of the mall at the World Trade Center in NYC the month before the 9/11 attacks, and still runs the new Westfield WTC mall, because not even unprecedented devastation can stop the company's drive to convert cities and towns into Westfield Shoppingtowns.

In 2018, the company merged with a giant European shopping mall operator to form Unibail-Rodamco-Westfield SE, the largest commercial real estate company in Europe, which will use the Westfield brand for most of its centres in the future. This new entity, with assets of €40 billion, still hasn't bothered to update the daggy old Westfield logo which has been in use since 1960.

White Night   1. A festival in Melbourne where many CBD buildings remain open all night, allowing residents and families to attend special arts events and discuss how liveable a city Melbourne is.

    2. An evening gathering of **Fraser Anning** supporters.

Wilson, Rebel A wonderful actress and human being, utterly above reproach, and nothing more will be said in case she sues.

Woop-woop A long way from anywhere. Though the term is generally applied to remote, uninhabited parts of Australia, it is most accurately used to refer to Adelaide.

— ***Welcome to Woop Woop*** Director Stephan Elliott's follow up to his smash hit *Priscilla, Queen of the Desert*. Cinemas screening it were also largely uninhabited.

Wowser A prude or killjoy. See **Shelton, Lyle**.

XYZ

Xenophobic Inexplicable

Yowie As there are regrettably no photos of them, here's a lovely picture of Yowie Bay in NSW *(J Bar)*

Xenophobic   Please explain?

XXXX   Australian for beer, as the company's ads state. More accurately, the full definition is 'Australian for a particular beer made in Queensland that nobody from any other state would be seen dead drinking'. Indeed, as far as people from other states are concerned, the XXXX signifies a swear word.

Yeah-nah   A polite way of clarifying or contradicting, while acknowledging that the speaker has understood the person they're speaking with, as in 'Yeah-nah, I don't think Pauline Hanson is the greatest political leader in Australian history.'

The phrase is also used to agree with a negative statement, such as 'Yeah-nah, **Sydney** really has been dead for years'.

Yidaki   A wind instrument made from a large, hollowed out log, originally invented by the Yolgnu people of Arnhem Land. No, don't call it a **didgeridoo**.

Yowie   1. A large, hairy, humanoid monster that's the Australian equivalent of the yeti or sasquatch.

2. A chocolate brand sold by Cadbury that featured a cartoon-like yowie. Though initially a huge hit, the product was eventually discontinued. Rumours persist that those involved were dragged away by a large ape-like creature that felt disrespected by the cutesy illustrations.

Zac A sixpence, which despite the onset of decimal currency, is still used in the phrase 'not worth a Zac'. The term can also be used to refer to Zac Efron's Australian accent in the movie *Mike and Dave Need Wedding Dates*, which is worth even less than 6p.

Zuytdorp The final entry in **Australia Post**'s alphabetical list of postcodes, Zuytdorp is named for a ship that was wrecked off the WA coast, and has a postcode of 6536. When viewed on Google Maps, there appears to be absolutely nothing there, making it indistinguishable from the rest of Western Australia.

ACKNOWLEDGEMENTS

My mother Linsay began working at the *Macquarie Dictionary* when it was in a tiny cottage in North Ryde and I was in primary school, and she spent many happy years there among the headwords. Consequently, I am privileged to have known most of the original team since childhood. Later in life, I very much enjoyed interviewing the former editor Sue Butler about Australian language on radio. Their project has been an extraordinary contribution to our culture, which I hope I haven't entirely disrespected with this book.

This dictionary also owes a debt to the ANU's Australian National Dictionary Centre's *Ozwords* and online list of the 'Meanings and origins of Australian words and idioms', which is full of discursive detail about many of the words contained in this dictionary, and well worth a read if you've ever wondered where, say, 'didgeridoo' came from.

As with everything I ever wonder idly about, I have also benefited greatly from the phenomenal resource that is Wikipedia.

With thanks to the fabulous team at Allen & Unwin, and immense gratitude as always to my family.

ABOUT THE AUTHOR

Dominic Knight was one of the excessively optimistic founding editors of *The Chaser*, a satirical newspaper launched in a tiny Glebe terrace in 1999. He became one of its destroyers in 2004 after the group belatedly acknowledged that newsprint had died several years earlier.

Since then he's been involved in most of the Chaser projects in print, stage, radio and television, and only got arrested that one time.

In a bid for respectability, Dom began presenting Evenings on ABC Radio Sydney and across NSW and the ACT in 2012. He left in 2016, and in 2017, returned to disreputability with Radio Chaser on Triple M.

Following several excessively semi-autobiographical novels, Dom released *Strayapedia*, a book devoted to the ironic celebration of his homeland, in 2017. In 2018, he followed it with *Trumpedia*, which detailed many of the bizarre scams involving the US president, such as his casinos, his vitamin pill business and his children.

Dom has also peddled opinions to the *Sydney Morning Herald*, *The Guardian*, *news.com.au*, *Rolling Stone*, *Cleo*, *Daily Life* and *The Drum*.

He lives in Sydney with his wife, daughter, dog and neuroses.

You may contact Dom at domknight.com, @domknight on Twitter or @dom_knight on Instagram, or simply catch him at Engadine Maccas on Grand Final night.

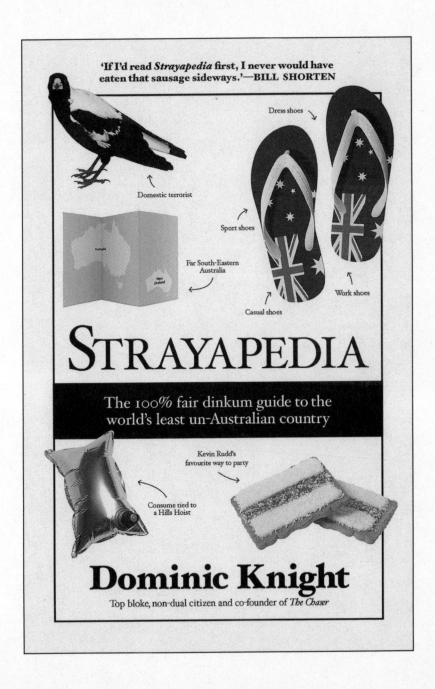

'If I'd read *Strayapedia* first, I never would have eaten that sausage sideways.'—BILL SHORTEN

Dress shoes

Domestic terrorist

Sport shoes

Far South-Eastern Australia

Work shoes

Casual shoes

STRAYAPEDIA

The 100% fair dinkum guide to the world's least un-Australian country

Kevin Rudd's favourite way to party

Consume tied to a Hills Hoist

Dominic Knight

Top bloke, non-dual citizen and co-founder of *The Chaser*